Unemployment and the Economists

Unemployment and the Economists

Edited by

Bernard Corry

Professor of Economics, Queen Mary and Westfield College, University of London, UK

Edward Elgar
Cheltenham, UK • Brookfield, US

Published by
Edward Elgar Publishing Limited
8 Lansdown Place
Cheltenham
Glos GL50 2HU
UK

Edward Elgar Publishing Company
Old Post Road
Brookfield
Vermont 05036
US

British Library Cataloguing in Publication Data
Unemployment and the economists
    1. Unemployment
    I.Corry, Bernard
    331.1'37

Library of Congress Cataloguing in Publication Data
Unemployment and the economists / edited by Bernard Corry.
    Papers presented at the History of Economics Spring Conference,
March 1995 at Gresham College, Holborn, London.
    Includes index.
    1. Unemployment — Congresses. 2. Employment (Economic theory) —
Congresses. I. Corry, Bernard.
    HD5707.5.U543   1996
    331.13'7—dc20   96–4213
                                                                              CIP

ISBN 1 85898 351 7

Typeset by Manton Typesetters, 5–7 Eastfield Road, Louth, Lincolnshire LN11 7AJ, UK.
Printed and bound in Great Britain by Hartnolls Limited, Bodmin, Cornwall

Contents

The authors

Alan Budd is Chief Economic Adviser to the Treasury and Head of the Government Economic Service. He is the author of *The Politics of Economic Planning* and has published numerous papers on the conduct of economic policy.

Bernard Corry is Emeritus Professor of Economics in the University of London at Queen Mary and Westfield College. He has published widely in the areas of labour economics and the history of economic thought and is the author of *Money, Saving and Investment in English Economics*.

Walter Eltis is Emeritus Fellow in Economics, Exeter College, Oxford, Gresham Professor of Commerce and Visiting Professor of Economics in the University of Reading. His books include *Britain's Economic Problems: Too Few Producers* (with Robert Bacon), *The Classical Theory of Economic Growth* and *Classical Economics, Public Expenditure and Growth*.

Jose Harris is Reader in Modern History at the University of Oxford and Fellow of St Catherine's College. Her books include *Unemployment and Politics 1886–1914*; *William Beveridge: A Biography*; and *Private Lives, Public Spirit. A Social History of Britain*. She was elected a Fellow of the British Academy in 1993.

Terry Peach is Senior Lecturer in Economics at the University of Manchester. He is the author of *Interpreting Ricardo* and has contributed widely to the understanding of classical economics.

George Peden is Professor of History at the University of Stirling. His books include *British Rearmament and the Treasury 1932–39* and *British Economic and Social Policy: Lloyd George to Margaret Thatcher*.

Preface

This volume consists of papers given at a conference held at Gresham College in March 1995. The conference was on the theme of unemployment and the economists and was attended by a distinguished group of economists and economic historians who have a particular interest in the development of economic ideas. It was sponsored by Gresham College and the History of Economic Thought Society and organized by Bernard Corry. The conference and this volume follow the highly successful 1994 conference, the papers from which were edited by Mark Blaug and published under the title *The Quantity Theory of Money: From Locke to Keynes and Friedman* (published by Edward Elgar 1995). I am sure that readers of the present volume will find that the high standards set by the earlier volume have been fully maintained.

The name Gresham does of course conjure up, primarily, a memory of discussions of monetary matters: concerns with debasement, inflation, and control of the money supply, but it is also useful to remember – as is pointed out in this volume – that the Tudor period also witnessed a concern for the unemployed and made suggestions for reducing their numbers.

This volume, with its contributions from Bernard Corry, Terry Peach, Jose Harris, George Peden, Alan Budd and Walter Eltis who is the current Gresham Professor of Commerce, traces the thoughts of writers on economic matters on the subject of unemployment, a topic which surely should be of equal or even more concern today than it was in the past!

PETER NAILOR
Gresham College
Barnard's Inn Hall
Holborn, London

It is with the deepest regret that the editor has to record that Professor Peter Nailor, Provost of Gresham College, died on 5 April 1996.

1. Unemployment in the history of economic thought: an overview and some reflections

Bernard Corry

Like all survey papers in economics, I shall deal in the currency of broad generalizations knowing only too well, especially in the company of scholars of economic thought and economic and social history, that there are many exceptions to these generalizations and in specific cases the exceptions may be of such a magnitude as to render the generalization otiose! Also like most surveys this one has relied heavily on previous surveys! In particular, I am especially indebted to the work of Garraty (1978), Harris (1972, 1977) and Hutchison (1988).

SOME PRELIMINARY WARNINGS FOR HISTORIANS OF ECONOMICS

What I have to say in this section concerns some health warnings that should be attached to all historical studies of economic inquiry; the subject matter of this chapter is but a salutary example of the need for these warnings. First, there is the problem of language; does the term unemployment as used today mean the same thing as, say, 200 years ago? Or perhaps different words were used to explain the same phenomenon; the actual term unemployment seems to have come into common use quite late in the day, but early phrases such as idleness or lack or want of employment may or may not be clear synonyms.

Search for the first use of a phrase or even the first statement of a theory may be a relatively harmless occupation, but it is not a particularly fruitful one.[1] The discovery of a new theory or approach is not necessarily its first statement but the first recognition that it is explaining something which had hitherto not been explicable. Giving a more coherent explanation to an existing phenomenon, 'money is spent until it is saved', is not really an early version of the Kahn–Keynes multiplier! Although after the event, i.e. the discovery of the Kahn–Keynes multiplier, it is easy to interpret earlier statements in the light of the new theory. But that is far from talking of an early discovery. We should only legitimately talk of originality when the idea, theory or framework is used to reinterpret an existing situation or to account for new facts (new situation).

Second, there is the difficult area of the relationship between the socio-economic structure and economic ideas. The importance given to unemployment in economic discourse and our interpretations of definitions, explanations and possible amelioration, will, at least partially, depend upon the stage of economic development, for example in contrasting pre-industrialized and industrialized societies. The problem has a social and political as well as an economic dimension to it. It is allied of course to our remarks about the interpretation of language. Is Josiah Child's argument that correct policy would ensure that 'Our mariners ... clothiers ... and all sorts of labouring people that depend on trade, will be more constantly and fully employed' (quoted Vickers, 1960, p. 22) to be interpreted in 20th-century terms? Does Francis Brewster's '(t)he full employment of all hands in the nation' (quoted Vickers, 1960, p. 22) mean the same as Beveridge? The answer seems to be a trivial no, but we have to approach with care. An economy in the early stages of industrialism with flexi hours[2] may still exhibit, for example, wide swings in the utilization of labour time, but these will show up as fluctuations in average hours worked rather than overt unemployment. In this case should we talk of the analysis of unemployment at such times?

The phenomenon of disguised unemployment in the development literature is another problem. An economy that does not exhibit overt unemployment may none the less have large portions of the work force in occupations with near-zero marginal productivity; now the general view is that these early statements are the reflection of growth problems, the capital stock being too low to ensure the full employment of a growing population. Hence, explanations of underemployment are commonly sought on the supply side rather than via aggregate demand failures. These situations of poverty in the midst of poverty are commonly distinguished from poverty in the midst of plenty. To put this question of structure into the present context, consider the view that the composition of the UK work force today has so altered that the concept of full employment has no proper meaning. The sort of evidence adduced is the rising proportion of part-time workers, the growth in self-employment and the increasing number of temporary and short-contract workers. These changes, it is said, force us to rethink the whole concept of full employment or even abandon the concept, and certainly must force a major rethink of employment policies. But it is not clear that these structural changes are at least partially a reflection of the overall shortfall in the demand for labour. The freeing or casualization of labour markets may make unemployment look different and even disguise it, but as with the 19th century it can still be a significant problem and may also require for its explanation, at least partially, some concern with aggregate demand failure.[3]

I have decided to organize this overview of the subject in the form of a series of questions. They are:

1. Historically, has unemployment been a subject of major concern to economists?
2. Has unemployment *in fact* been a major factor in the process of capitalist economic development?
3. Who or what is to blame for unemployment? And as part of this question and one that has had major significance in the historical literature, what is the significance of the distinction between voluntary and involuntary unemployment?
4. What policy prescriptions have economists advocated to deal with the problem of unemployment?

Clearly these questions are highly interrelated and there are of course several more that we could reasonably ask in a more extended treatment.

A CAUSE FOR CONCERN?

Have discussions of unemployment in any of its many facets been of major concern to economists in their deliberations? Have there been periodic peaks of interest interspersed with other periods of lack of interest in the topic? If this has been the case, is this periodicity connected with the economic cycle of boom and slump? Has unemployment been a prime cause of concern for economists?

It may be a consequence of my sheltered background but I have to confess that I have never met an unemployed economist. I have met those who may be classified as being in the category 'paid labour hoarding' but none who is actively seeking work and unable to find it. I am sure there must be some and perhaps my sample is the unrepresentative one of academia. And, may I add, today I rarely meet, from any walk of life, those who are voluntarily unemployed! I make these remarks only semi-frivolously because what hits me most on reading a sample of the relevant literature, and perhaps the major conclusion that one is forced to accept on studying what economists or writers on economic matters have had to say about unemployment generally including, *inter alia*, its definition, classification, causes, and cures (if the latter is deemed an appropriate end of policy), is the rather complacent attitude towards unemployment adopted in the writings. This is more true of what may be termed 'academic' writing than that of 'amateurs'.[4] The degree of complacency does of course vary with the immediate circumstances, but by and large economists have tended to regard unemployment as an inevitable concomitant of free market systems and in many cases have regarded its existence as a symptom of Pareto optimality, by which I mean that it is often regarded as a voluntary, individual maximizing act even when there is job rationing. A perennial question among economists has always been: 'Do the poor want to work? (Goodwin, 1972). Allied to this complacency is a general scepticism and often outright denial of the efficacy of any plans to reduce unemployment unless they are compatible with the profit-seeking activities of the entrepreneurial class. 'You can't do it' or 'It won't achieve the results you meant' have been and still are the typical responses to plans to increase employment that do not involve wage cuts or productivity increases.

There are some major exceptions to this rather matter of fact, it's part of life, attitude towards unemployment. I now list, with a few brief comments on each, these periods of concern when there seems to have been a particular bubbling-up of literature on questions of unemployment.

Pre-Classical Thought

Here we enter into the endless debate about the 'Keynesian' element in mercantilist thought.[5] There are many issues involved in the debate and we shall refer to these in a moment, but it does seem to be clear that, at least in late 17th- and early 18th-century literature, there was a concern with unemployed members of the population. It was, of course, Keynes who brought back to the so-called mercantilist literature a fame and importance that had been taken from it by the triumph of English classical political economy (Keynes, 1936, 1973, chapter 23). This view has been broadened by writers, like Vickers (1960) and Coleman (1977), into the one that full employment was *the* major focus of mercantilist economic policy. Certainly, apt quotations may be found from the literature to bolster Keynes's claim in the penultimate chapter of the *General Theory* (1936), but historians of thought have been somewhat loath to jump on the bandwagon. There are several reasons for this:

1. Some of the discussions of unemployment related to workers' leisure preferences and the alleged existence of a backward bending supply curve of labour.[6] We shall deal later with the interminable disputes about the distinction between voluntary and involuntary unemployment, let us just for the moment say that the voluntary unemployed are those who reject work at existing wage rates and that the involuntarily unemployed are those who are job rationed at existing wage rates. Now some of the discussions of idleness relate to the voluntary withdrawal of labour. An

apt example of this is to be found in Berkeley's *The Querist* (1735, 1891) where he complains of the Irish agricultural labourers' refusal to work a full working week.

2. With regard to Keynesian-type thought in this period, the obvious points have to be made that the role of investment either at home or abroad via a balance of payments surplus (an apparent aim of policy) was minimal in an essentially agricultural-based economy with little fixed capital equipment, and where the labour force consisted primarily of agricultural labourers and menial servants rather than industrial factory-based workers.

3. As an extension of (2) above, much unemployment and underemployed labour seems to have been due to seasonal factors and bad harvests.

4. No actual statement, however primitive, of a theory of effective demand can be found in the existing literature.

5. Plausible explanations of observed, involuntary, unemployment may be given via a combination of wage inflexibility and geographical labourer immobility.

But whether or not a Keynesian-type explanation is plausible, there can be no question that the existence of unemployment as an important economic and social issue stands out clearly in the literature as does the demands that government do something about it.

The Classical Period

It is tempting to argue that there was another intense period of cause for concern after 1815. Certainly, reams have been written on the debates about the post-Napoleonic War depression and especially the Ricardo–Malthus controversy.[7] It is also clear that the focus of classical economics was on problems of growth and development rather than efficiency in a static allocation sense, although too much should not be made of this emphasis as compared with marginalist writers. But it would be wrong to say that discussions of unemployment are central to mainstream classical thought. After what was at the time a rather minor skirmish between Ricardo and Malthus, discussions of unemployment did not loom large in the standard literature; for example in textbooks such as those by Mill (1848, 1966) or Fawcett (1863) there is barely a reference to the subject. Poverty and its causes and possible remedies did engage the classical literature but their concerns here were mainly with low-earned incomes – often due to the casualization of labour – and those incapable of work rather than the unemployed as such. Much-disputed issues include: how far we can blame this lack of concern on classical macroeconomics with its, implicit at least, assumption of full employment and labour markets that cleared; how far did it mirror economic reality; or how far did it reflect the lack of empirical evidence of the actual facts about labour markets. But I believe it is fair to say, as a broad generalization, that the unemployment problem was not high on the economists' agenda during the classical period.

The 1880s

It seems to be the case, and here I lean heavily on the investigations of Harris (1972), that it was in the 1880s and 1890s that the question of poverty began to be disentangled from the question of unemployment,[8] and the 'able-bodied' poor were separated from those incapable of sustaining themselves and their dependence by gainful employment. The distinction between voluntary and involuntary unemployment – although as we shall see, not in the Keynesian sense – comes into the economists' terminology. Poverty studies give a much more detailed picture of the contribution of unemployment to distress among the working classes and a serious debate about the costs and benefits of unemployment insurance comes into the literature. There was much agreement with Foxwell's (1886) comment that: 'uncertainty of employment seems to me to demand the first place in the attention of the friends of social progress and of the claims of labour'. Or with Marshall's (1923, 1965, pp. 260–1) remark:

> Forced interruption to labour is a grievous evil. Those whose livelihood is secure, gain physical and mental health from happy and well-spent holidays. But want of work, with long continued anxiety, consumes a man's best strength without any return. His wife becomes thin; and his children get, as it were, a nasty notch in their lives, which is perhaps never overgrown.

This increased concern was not primarily expressed by professional economists, rather there was growing public awareness of the problem. This is evidenced in the contributions on the subject to literary journals, socio-economic investigations and the like. Pears even awarded a prize for the best contribution to the subject![9] Much of the economists' contributions were made up of quite detailed accounts of the facts about the lives of the unemployed. The distinction that we have today – due perhaps to professional specialization – between what may loosely be termed the social and economic aspects of unemployment was not made.

The Age of Keynes: Full Employment is Here to Stay!

Another period of concern – perhaps *the* period – was of course the Keynesian era. Unemployment or rather its flip side, full employment, was on the lips of most orthodox economists, especially during World War II and for about 20 years after. But on the whole this sustained interest, evidenced in the volume of journal articles, books and government and semi-governmental reports devoted to it, is an exception in the broad history of the overworld, as contrasted with the underworld, of economics. It was exceptional for various complex reasons which may be listed as (although not in order of importance):

1. The recent memories of the world slump with unemployment figures above 20 per cent of the work force in several countries made unemployment a central social fact.
2. Wartime and immediate post-war propaganda in the allied countries, especially the UK and USA, emphasized full employment as a major object of government policy after the war. This was to be contrasted, it was promised, especially in the UK, with the experiences of demobbed ex-service personnel post-1918.
3. Not merely did governments promise 'homes for heroes' but also 'jobs for heroes' – they also thought they knew how to achieve it. They had been offered and bought Keynesian economics. For the first time the economics profession with one or two important exceptions[10] was united in accepting the Keynesian model and the policy implication that there was a strong and positive role for government in employment policy.
4. These Keynesian policies seemed, at first blush at least, to be perfectly compatible with the interests and inspirations of capital[11] and indeed a fully employed economy was seen as one that would enhance the volume if not the share of profits in national income. It was only later that the inexorable rise in governments' expenditure in all free market economies, and objections to the allegedly high levels of taxation – egged on by the infamous Laffer curve[12] led to the revolt of the chattering classes against welfarism and the nanny state.

The Present Climate

I have the distinct impression that, currently, unemployment has gone from the headlines among professional economists, but it does of course depend on where you live, where you work, and who you talk to. It may be the improving economic situation where indices of employment, growth, balance of payments and exchange rates are used; it may be that economists have exhausted their ingenuity in dreaming up solutions other than the rather tired cry for retraining and skill improvement. By and large, economists have accepted some version of the natural rate/NAIRU hypothesis and look basically to supply-side considerations which harp back to solutions of bygone days. There is little here for Yummies![13] So the ball is back in the workers' court.

A brief word about gender and unemployment concern. Most discussion has, at least until recently, taken place within the context of the unemployment of 'prime males'. This may have had some justification in the heyday of industrialism when most prime males were full-time workers and most, although by no means all, women in paid employment were part-time or seasonal workers and were classified in the economics of labour literature as secondary workers. The problem was then seen to be to explain cyclical and secular patterns in female activity rates. But in the post-industrial age, with, for example, women making up nearly 50 per cent of the working population in the UK and an increasing proportion of men in the part-time, temporary and self-employed categories, it is clear that reputable studies of unemployment have to include women on a par with men.[14]

HAS UNEMPLOYMENT ACTUALLY BEEN A PROBLEM?

Now, against this allegation of lack of concern by economists about unemployment, it is argued that this apparent general lack of interest, except in times of severe slump, merely reflects the fact that over the long haul in the development of industrial and pre-industrial capitalism, unemployment has not been a major problem compared with the traditional economists' concerns – *pace* Robbins's definition of our subject – with questions of efficiency, allocation and the growth of income per head.

Is it true that the record of history tells us that (just talking about the so-called economic cost) the loss of output due to the under-utilization of labour time would not show up on our long-term trend curves? Was Kaldor (1960) right to express surprise that the system had run so close to full employment? Actually evaluating the historical record of the extent of unemployment is an exercise fraught with difficulties and controversy and a complex research area in its own right.[15] Definition and measurement is difficult enough today in a world of sophisticated surveys, but attempts to look backwards – especially before national insurance records – are subject to massive measurement errors. But given data limitations what does the record of history show about unemployment? Has the secular growth path of capitalism been close to a full employment path so that intervention has been unnecessary, or is the record one of persistent under-utilization of labour? The question of evidence becomes even more complicated if one looks at the regional spread of unemployment and relates it to definitions and theories of structural unemployment. For example, it seems to have been the case, and I believe it still is the received wisdom, that pre-1914 unemployment in the UK was prevalent in the south, with London in particular being the major problem. In the south, industrial production had failed to keep pace with the growth of population and this contrasted with the north where traditional industries were located and were growing rapidly. World War I was a watershed and produced a complete reversal of the pre-war pattern – so goes the received wisdom. But recent research, using more micro-based data, has cast grave doubts on this view and hence may well force a revision of our explanations of unemployment in that era (see, e.g., Southall, 1988).

Suppose the record of history is patchy and unemployment has not trended at full employment. Is this failure to be laid at the door of the economics profession? Economists have often complained that they are not in control of policy and hence cannot be pilloried for the failures of the economic system to create jobs for all. Economists make far too much of this line of defence, particularly in more recent times. Governments' attempts at employment policy, including the familiar cry that intervention will worsen things, have always found contemporary support among one group of economists or the other, and certainly in the UK what governments have tended to do has coincided with majority economic opinion.[16]

The complacency referred to above arises I believe partially because economists, like everyone else, get used to a certain state of affairs and begin to accept it as the norm. This, perhaps inevitably, means that it ceases to be the centre of interest and hence intellectual effort is devoted elsewhere. The history of economic inquiry is littered with examples of economists confusing the current situation with a permanent or semi-permanent shift in the economic structure. A short-term, post-1946 dollar shortage becomes the chronic dollar gap; a period of mass unemployment in the 1930s becomes secular stagnation; a short period of low unemployment (1950–70) becomes why full employment is here to stay; a short period of stagflation becomes the end of trade-off theory; a combination of high unemployment and economic growth (today) becomes the secular rise in the natural or NAIRU rate of unemployment and so on.

WHO OR WHAT IS TO BLAME?

Another important feature of the broad historical discussions is the apportionment of blame. How have economists apportioned blame? Who or what have been the main culprits in sustaining and or creating unemployment? To this issue we now turn.

I will start with a broad generalization which I am sure some of you will find contentious – but that is another feature of generalizations. It is this; with very few exceptions the blame for the existence, or, perhaps more exactly, the persistence of unemployment has been placed squarely on the heads of workers in general for their failure to respond to conditions of job rationing, by which I mean an excess supply of labour at existing wage rates, by a reduction in wages. Rarely have economists blamed the workers for initiating an increase in unemployment – this has usually been laid at the door of 'impersonal' real or monetary disturbances. Whether or not these initiating causes have been due to human folly in terms of perverse policies or due to endogenous forces within the logic of market capitalism has been much debated, but the follow up, to repeat, has invariably been the fact that workers can ameliorate their employment prospects by wage reduction. The causes have been varied, the analyses sometimes crude and sometimes sophisticated but the commonality is quite clear, as are the exceptions. From the quite crude analysis of the wages fund to the current theory of the determinants of the NAIRU, a reduction in wages was the way to decrease unemployment. Analytically, the overwhelming method of analysis has been to set up a model of a labour market with the standard properties of a commodity auction market. When this auction market fails to predict reality, rigidities are appealed to to square the evidence.[17] In this sense, it is the actions of self-interested rational individuals that have imposed stickiness on wages and prices so that in the modern literature we have the concept of voluntary job rationing. This tale of 'it's your own fault' winds its way through the centuries. It had long been surmised that money wages were less flexible than prices, so the dance of prices around wages brought periodic rises in real wages not due to increases in productivity, and excess supplies of labour presaged a rise in unemployment until wages adjusted or reached their appropriate level. Whatever the possible cause of this inflexibility of money wages the cure was always the same – increase the downward flexibility of wages. How this was to be achieved, we shall briefly consider in a moment.

NOBODY'S TO BLAME – IT'S A TRADE-OFF!

The idea that there might be a negative trade-off between the goal of reducing unemployment and other desirable ends of policy has been another plank in the campaign to take out unemployment as the major policy issue. The main trade-off discussed in the literature has been that between unemployment and the rate of inflation. The idea had been around for some time; references could (possibly) be made to Marx (1867, 1976), Fisher (1926), Keynes (1936), and Brown (1955) but its popularization was undoubtedly due to Phillips (1958). The result of his analysis and its subsequent development[18] and elaboration was to suggest that we had a choice between levels of the two variables, and the social optimum would be a function of (a) the trade-off curve, and (b) the subjective, social rate of substitution between them. Within this framework the goal of full employment could still be aimed for but we might instead choose a compromise solution. As Britton (1994) recently stated: 'Society has given up the aim of full employment because it found the cost in terms of other objectives was too great'. In the current literature, full employment is barely indexed; it has been replaced with equilibrium employment or its apparent equivalents – the natural rate or NAIRU rate of unemployment.

CLASSIFYING UNEMPLOYMENT

Attempts to classify unemployment into types and to relate these different types to apparently different causes has been a major feature of the literature. The initial formal attempt seems to have come in the late 19th century, although there are hints of it in the earlier literature. For example, consider the post-1815 situation in the UK. The initial orthodox response to post-war unemployment was, as exemplified in the works of Ricardo (1821, 1951–1955, p. 265), to regard the problem as structural in the sense that it was compounded of unplanned demobilization and a switch in demand from war industries to peace-time activities. This involved both industrial, occupational and locational problems for the labour force. Later economists tried to distinguish cyclical and non-cyclical unemployment; cyclical unemployment had in a way always been recognized since the day that periodical movements in broad aggregates had been seen to be a concomitant of capitalist economic development. Fluctuations in income and employment or, to use Hawtrey's (1913) phrase, 'good and bad trade', begin to be discussed in earnest in the early classical period although the major emphasis remains on output fluctuations rather then the resultant employment fluctuations. In general – and this may have been a reflection of reality – the general vision was of output and hence employment growing trendwise at full utilization[19] with the labour market clearing in good times but with signs of job rationing in bad times. The notion that there might be involuntary unemployment (we shall discuss the possible meanings of that electrifying term in the next two sections) in periods of relative prosperity, and that this unemployment had to do with the changing pattern of demand and the inevitable lags in the restructuring of industry, did not become prominent until after World War I and is commonly held to be a reflection of the actual progress of the economies involved.

THE DISTINCTION BETWEEN VOLUNTARY AND INVOLUNTARY UNEMPLOYMENT – ALL HEAT AND NO LIGHT?

The Origins of the Term Involuntary Unemployment

One of the major areas of discussion and dispute in the literature on unemployment has been the alleged distinction between voluntary and involuntary unemployment. Its primacy in the literature was undoubtedly due to its treatment by Keynes but its usage predates him as we shall see. Currently, severe doubts are expressed about the utility of the distinction. We must now investigate this matter.

The distinction between voluntary and involuntary unemployment has existed in the literature since about the last quarter of the 19th century. There has always been much confusion over the meaning of the two terms and possible explanations for their relative existences. As in the past, opinion today is much divided as to the value of the distinction. For example, recent opinion seems to favour the dropping of the terms from the economists' vocabulary.[20]

The term involuntary unemployment does not seem to have come into common usage by economists until the 20th century, indeed the actual use of the terms 'unemployed' or 'unemployment' are only beginning to make their *common* appearance towards the middle of the 19th century. Thomas Attwood (quoted in Corry, 1962, p. 86), famed for his involvement in the Birmingham currency school, did define full employment as early as 1832 but much of the early discussion of the topic was in terms of the under-utilization of capital – factories lying idle – and the distress involved was related from a capitalists' viewpoint rather than directly focused on the unemployment of labour. Until the 1880s, the major social policy concern of economists, certainly in the UK and USA, was with the problem of poverty. The economic miracle of growth that had brought such prosperity to the Victorian business and professional classes, had trickled through to skilled workers but had left vast reservoirs of poverty. Initially, this poverty was not seen to be directly connected with unemployment; there may originally have been good grounds for this view, many in work were below measured poverty lines and many not in the labour force were in the same situation.

Explanations of unemployment tended to be in terms of what may be called a characteristics theory of unemployment,[21] an approach incidentally that has resurfaced at regular intervals in the literature of unemployment, not least in current discussion. Characteristics theory lays emphasis on personal characteristics of the unemployed; their failure to develop a capitalistic work ethic, their ill-health, lack of any or appropriate skill training, etc. Public concern was expressed at this state of affairs but any suggestions of public aid for the unemployed was dismissed with the view that it would inevitably worsen the situation. As Harris (1972, pp. 1–2), in her comprehensive study of the late Victorian and Edwardian period, has put the matter:

> Public employment and public relief for the unemployed were therefore regarded as both dangerous and futile; and lack of employment was seen either as a voluntary condition which working men incurred wilfully, or as an inevitable occurrence which they should predict and provide for out of their earnings whilst in employment.

But by the end of the 1880s, mainly due to the clear evidence produced by surveys of poverty, the famous examples being those of Booth (1902, 1969) and Rowntree (1901), unemployment analyses began to be disentangled from the general poverty issue and indeed could be said to have taken over, or at least were on a par with it, as the major social problem to be investigated by economic inquirers. It is at this time that the terms 'unemployed' and 'unemployment' began to be used more frequently, although we still have phrases like want of employment, work-shortage, non-employment, involuntary idleness, and other euphemisms. Efforts were also made to measure unemployment and this inevitably involved more careful thought being given to exactly what was the meaning of unemployment. In the UK, until the introduction of unemployment insurance in 1908, the only available measure of the unemployed was that taken from trade unions' records of payments to unemployed members, and generalizations formed from records relating to the whole working population. This procedure brought in severe estimation biases as contemporary commentators were well aware.

Hobson argued that we should try to estimate the numbers of unemployed 'by the inclusion of all forms of involuntary leisure suffered by the working classes' (1895, p. 419). Later on, in the same contribution, he actually uses the term 'involuntary unemployment' (p. 420). He also points out that the figure so estimated will differ from those obtained from trade unions' estimates.

Sidney and Beatrice Webb in their *Prevention of Destitution* (1911), following very much the analysis and recommendations of the *Minority Report of the Poor Law Commission*, advocated as an anti-destitution policy, 'a national policy dealing with every aspect of the problem, which, if deliberately pursued and experimentally developed, will progressively operate so as more and more to prevent the very occurrence of Involuntary Unemployment' (p. 107). This unemployment involved the 'dismissal of thousands of workmen, for absolutely no fault or shortcoming of their own (Ibid., p. 111), and note that these dismissals were not due to adverse personal characteristics, choice, or changes in the structure of production; they were due to a general depression of trade 'which seems to operate quite irrespective of seasonal fluctuations, industrial revolutions, or personal shortcomings' (Ibid., p. 111). On the other hand, those workers who chose to be unemployed should receive no public support, indeed should be positively deterred. In the words of the Webbs again, 'it is essential, on grounds of economy, that there should be a searching out of all incipient cases and such a disciplinary supervision as will prevent persons from becoming destitute through neglected infancy, neglected childhood, preventable illness, and voluntary unemployment' (Ibid., p. 317).

There is clear evidence of the use of the term in Cambridge economics before World War I. Pigou (1913, p. 14) uses the term freely: 'unemployment does not include all the idleness of wage-earners, but only that part of it which is, from their point of view and in the existing conditions at the time, involuntary'. Those excluded from his definition are 'those who are idle, not from necessity, but from choice' (Ibid., p. 14). In modern terminology, Pigou was defining involuntary unemployment as the difference – strictly measured in terms of hours of labour – between the supply and demand for labour at the current real wage. As Pigou (Ibid., p. 16) put the matter:

> the amount of unemployment ... which exists in any industry is measured by the number of hours' work ... by which the employment of the persons 'attached to' or 'occupied in' that industry falls short of the number of hours' work that these persons would have been willing to provide at the current rate of wages under current conditions of employment.

D.H. Robertson, whose thoughts on monetary economics were so intertwined with those of Keynes – at least until the *Treatise on Money* – also makes use of the concept of involuntary unemployment. This occurs in his *A Study of Industrial Fluctuation* (1915, 1948, p. 209), where we read:

> For while an employer cannot easily compel a workman to work more than he wishes to, he can, through his control of the access to the instruments of production, effectually prevent him from working as much as he wishes to. It follows that the complaints of involuntary unemployment among the wage-earners need not make us doubt the correctness, as far as concerns the business classes, and therefore the course of industrial policy, of our diagnosis of the industrial malady.

Again the Webbs, writing this time in 1929, state that 'Involuntary Unemployment is now a world-wide constant phenomenon in every industrial state'. And along the lines of their earlier use of the term they mean by involuntary unemployment the inability immediately to find work.

We have shown so far that the term involuntary unemployment was commonly used in the literature relating to unemployment prior to the 1930s. Although there is some ambiguity in the use of the term, it generally relates to what would today count as the Labour Force Survey definition of unemployment, that is to say those out of work who are actively seeking work at the current wage rate and are available immediately for work.[22] That is what most people would think of as a reasonable definition of unemployment. This way of looking at involuntary unemployment is very common in current interpretations of Keynes's economics.[23] But how in fact did Keynes use the term and how did he account for its existence? To these questions we now turn, for it is here that the great muddle begins.

Keynes and Involuntary Unemployment

We must spend what might appear to be a disproportionate amount of time on this section of our survey. This is for several reason: first, to clarify what Keynes actually argued, especially with reference to involuntary unemployment and its cause and cure. Much current interpretation and especially the analytics of what is termed 'New Keynesianism' is far wide of the mark of what 'Keynes's economics' was all about. Second, Keynes was clearly opposed to perfectionist theories of the persistence of unemployment. And third, he squarely places the blame for (large scale) unemployment on the economic system and not the workers.

From his earliest writings, Keynes was concerned with what was later to be called macroeconomic issues, but there is not much in his academic work before the *General Theory* that is *explicitly* focused on unemployment as opposed to fluctuations in economic activity in general. His paper on fluctuations given in 1913 to the Political Economy Club is mainly concerned with what he calls 'financial fluctuations' and barely refers to output or employment (Keynes, 1913, 1973, pp. 2–14). In *A Tract on Monetary Reform* published in 1923, Keynes is primarily trying to explain fluctuations in the general level of prices, the Wicksellian-type model that he uses to conduct his analysis puts the cause of most examples of macroeconomic instability at the door of price fluctuations: 'Unemployment, the precarious life of the worker, the disappointment of expectation, the sudden loss of saving, the excess windfalls to individuals, the speculator, the profiteer – all proceed, in large measure, from the instability of the standard of value' (Keynes, 1923, 1971, p. 5). There is little overt concern with the situation of the unemployed in periods of depression: 'the period of depression has exacted its penalty from the working classes more in the form of unemployment than by a lowering of real wages, and State assistance to the unemployed has greatly moderated even this penalty' (ibid., p. 28).

In *A Treatise on Money* (Keynes, 1930, 1971), Keynes is still mainly concerned with the effects of changes in the general price level caused by divergences between saving and investment. A fall in the general price level creates a problem because labour costs do not fall in line with commodity prices, they only adjust with a time lag and it is for this reason that we observe output and employment fluctuations in the face of price fluctuations. The analysis here is very classical, at least in the sense that it does imply that money wage stickiness is the factor that leads to output and employment fluctuations rather than just fluctuations in the general price level. Keynes writes:

> the entrepreneur, faced with prices falling faster than costs, had three alternatives open to him – to put up with his losses as best he could; to withdraw from his less profitable activities, thus reducing output and employment; to embark on a struggle with his employees to reduce their money earnings per unit of output – of which only the last was capable of restoring real equilibrium from the national point of view. (Keynes, 1930, 1971, p. 163)

He further argues that long periods of unemployment were caused by the difficulty of lowering 'money-earnings per unit of the factors of production', we often have to wait for 'increases in efficiency' to 'lower money-earnings per unit of output'. We make this point about the classical nature of Keynes's diagnosis of unemployment in the *Treatise* because we wish to bring out in starkest contrast his new approach in the *General Theory* and with it the key role of the 'Keynesian' concept of involuntary unemployment. It is not without interest that in the monumental *Encyclopaedia of the Social Sciences* published in 1935, the long article on unemployment contributed by Karl Pribram does not mention Keynes nor is there reference to him in the extensive bibliography. But of course a lot was happening to Keynes's thinking between the *Treatise* and the publication of the *General Theory* in 1936. In terms of economic events, the beginning of the world recession began with the New York stock market crash of 24 October 1929, although the world implications were not immediately recognized. At about the same time the *Treatise* was sent to the printers.

Also, at the same time in early November 1929, Phillip Snowden, Chancellor of the Exchequer in the Labour government, set up the Macmillan Committee to investigate the monetary and financial system of the UK; Keynes was a member of the committee and gave evidence before it. Then, in January 1930, the government set up the Economic Advisory Council of which Keynes was also a member and to that body was soon added a Committee of Economists which Keynes chaired.[24]

In his work for these bodies we have an ongoing record both of the changing analytical framework and the policy implications that this changing framework involved; what is clear is that Keynes displays increasing scepticism about the efficacy of a general reduction in money wages in lessening mass unemployment. His earlier arguments that a general reduction in wages would be difficult to engineer, are beginning to be reinforced by the possibility that even if the reduction were possible, it would not lessen unemployment. This position is strengthened once Keynes finally drops the analysis of the *Treatise* and works in terms of the model of the *General Theory*. To consider this point we have to take a stand on the essential break between the macro-analysis of the *Treaties* and other of Keynes's writings using that framework, and the analysis of the *General Theory*. Only then will the crucial importance of the concept of involuntary unemployment be apparent. As we shall seek to demonstrate, it is not a throwaway concept or marginal to the main structure. It is, however, fraught with difficulties of interpretation as commentators have long realized, but to jettison the concept, as many economists argue today, is to miss the central point of the *General Theory*. We may have legitimate grounds, theoretical and empirical, for rejecting the economics of the *General Theory*, in part or in total, but essential to any understanding of it is the concept of involuntary unemployment – more even than the analytic framework. Keynes was perhaps the first major economist to *absolve the involuntary unemployed from blame for their state*.[25]

Briefly, the main differences between the analysis of the *Treatise* and the *General Theory* are:

1. the spelling out of a theory of effective demand;
2. the determination of equilibrium output (and hence equilibrium employment) where aggregate demand equalled aggregate supply;
3. the argument that the equilibrium so determined was stable;
4. the argument that the equilibrium was not necessarily at full employment.[26]

In summary, the central new feature of the *General Theory* is that, given supply conditions, equilibrium output is determined by effective demand, and this output is often at less than full employment output. So far, so good! But, for purposes of comparison with contemporary thinking, Keynes's problem was to translate this theory into orthodox classical labour market analysis. This is where the problem began. Perhaps Keynes should never have attempted such a translation. Now where does the concept of involuntary unemployment come in? If equilibrium output is below full employment output (a concept that can be fraught with ambiguous interpretation), then employment will be below full employment. The unemployment that this causes, Keynes called involuntary unemployment. It is involuntary because it has not been caused by personal characteristics, by trade union activity, by structural imbalance, or government legislation, but by aggregate demand failure.

The new ideas in the *General Theory* did not, of course, appear overnight; Keynes went through a long period of modifying or rather, throwing over the structure of the *Treatise* to come up with his revolutionary ideas. The process by which he did this has been well documented in the literature and we here follow the interpretation pioneered by Patinkin (1982) whose narration seems to fit best all the available facts. The actual term involuntary unemployment only makes its appearance in Keynes late in the day – in rough drafts of the *General Theory* – that date from 1932 (see Rymes, 1989). It was after he had discovered the theory of effective demand and worked out its implications for Say's Law and the classical emphasis on voluntary unemployment.

Who is to Blame? Involuntary Unemployment in the *General Theory*

Keynes sought to absolve workers from the crime of unemployment. His very use of the term involuntary was not *just* meant in a technical, analytic sense but it was also meant to convey Keynes's fundamental break with tradition – what he rightly or wrongly called the classical tradition – that the unemployed had any responsibility for their plight. Responsibility here is in the sense that it was in their power to take measures that would reduce the level of unemployment.

The term first makes its appearance in chapter 2. We should recall here that after publication of the *General Theory*, Keynes stated that this was the section of his book most in need of revision. He discusses the classical postulate that, 'the utility of the wage when a given volume of labour is employed is equal to the marginal disutility of that amount of labour' (Keynes, 1936, 1973, p. 6), original emphasis. He notes the modifications necessary for imperfect competition in labour markets and remarks that this postulate is compatible with 'voluntary' unemployment:

> For a realistic interpretation of it legitimately allows for various inexactnesses of adjustment which stand in the way of continuous full employment: for example, unemployment due to a temporary want of balance between the relative quantities of specialised resources as result of miscalculation or intermittent demand; or to time lags consequent on unforeseen changes; or to the fact that the change-over from one employment to another cannot be effected without a certain delay, so that there will always exist in a non-static society a proportion of resources unemployed 'between jobs'. (Keynes, 1936, 1973, p. 6)

But even this is not the sum of voluntary unemployment! We read further that:

> (in) addition ... the postulate is also compatible with 'voluntary' unemployment due to the refusal or inability of legislation or social practices or of a combination for collective bargaining or of a slow response to change or of mere human obstinacy, to accept a reward corresponding to the value of the product attributable to its marginal productivity. (Ibid. p. 6)[27]

This is quite a list and takes us well beyond frictional and structural unemployment; it clearly is meant to include what we today would discuss under the headings of trade union monopoly models; insider/outsider models; efficient wage theory, and the like. So what category is left for his new theory of unemployment? 'The classical postulates do not admit of the possibility of the third category, which I shall define ... as "involuntary" unemployment' (Ibid., p. 6). Notice at this stage that Keynes's earlier explanation of the persistence of unemployment after a shock, that it was due to wage inflexibility or lags in the adjustment of money wages to a fall in prices, is now part of voluntary unemployment. *So that we do not now have the equating of involuntary unemployment with all those seeking work, willing to work, and unable to find it.* This was the typical meaning given to the term by earlier writers – Cambridge and otherwise. The change in emphasis reflects Keynes's other major policy change from the *Treatise* to the *General Theory*. He *no longer believes in the efficacy of wage reductions (even if politically possible) as a remedy for mass unemployment.*

So how does Keynes define involuntary unemployment? The ambiguities and misunderstandings that have plagued the interpretation of the concept begin with Keynes's famous and admittedly rather tortuous definition. It bears repeating in full because here is the origin of the post-*General Theory* part of the story:

> Men are involuntarily unemployed if, in the event of a small rise in the price of wage-goods relatively to the money-wage, both the aggregate supply of labour willing to work for the current money-wage and the aggregate demand for it at that wage would be greater than the existing volume of employment. (Ibid., p. 15, original emphasis)

He goes on to state that this definition, which we shall interpret shortly, is the 'same thing' as his other one which looks at involuntary unemployment as full employment minus actual unemployment. Full employment is defined as 'a situation in which aggregate employment is inelastic in response to an increase in the effective demand for its output' (Ibid., p. 26). Let us return to that first definition. A standard interpretation of it is to translate the quoted passage into a neo-classical model of the labour market; it is usual to write:

$$N_d = f(W/P): f' < 0 \qquad (1.1)$$

$$N_s = f(W/P): f' > 0 \qquad (1.2)$$

$$N_d = N_s \qquad (1.3)$$

$$*W/P = f(N_d - N_s): f' > 0 \qquad (1.4)$$

Where N_d and N_s are the demand and supply of labour, W is the money wage rate, P is 'the' price level assuming for simplicity that the same price is applicable to both demand and supply functions, $*W/P$ is the rate of change of the real wage, and f' refers to the relevant derivative.

Equation 1.1 is the demand for labour derived from standard cost-minimizing behaviour; equation (1.2) is the labour supply, strictly speaking it should be for hours (as should the demand function) but if we assume a fixed working week we may interpret it in terms of number of workers; equation (1.3) is the market clearing; and equation (1.4) is the market adjustment.

It would seem to follow from this framework, using the analytics of orthodox price theory, that a situation where $N_s > N_d$ or in Keynes's words where 'The existing real equivalent of (the money) wage exceeds the marginal disutility of the existing employment' (Ibid., p. 14) can only represent either (a) a temporary situation as wages fall to clear the market, or (b) that wages are inflexible downwards and the disequilibrium will persist.[28] Involuntary unemployment then becomes a symptom of wages being 'too high'. But this interpretation is most emphatically not what Keynes intended. His many policy statements make this clear, beyond doubt, but the ambiguity in interpretation has arisen because of Keynes's apparent acceptance of the first classical postulate, that, to repeat it, 'the wage is equal, to the marginal product of labour' (Ibid., p. 5). Commentators have interpreted this as a belief in the classical demand function for labour, with employment as a function of the real wage. Hence, in order to show any difference at all between Keynes's vision of the labour market and that depicted in classical economic reasoning, it has been assumed that the difference must lie in the treatment of labour supply. Keynes gave credence to this way of thinking by his alleged acceptance of the first postulate. What did Keynes have to say about labour demand in the *General Theory*? Well in a very real sense that is what the whole of the book is about! But let us be more specific. The first thing to be clear about is that he did assume short-run falling marginal product to labour, from this it followed, in his simplified economy, that there was a negative relationship between employment and the real wage. This is what Keynes meant by accepting the first postulate; as he elucidated his acceptance further he stated, '(i)t means that, with a given organization, equipment and technique, real wages and the volume of output (and hence of employment) are uniquely correlated, so that, in general, an increase in employment can only occur to the accompaniment of a decline in the rate of real wages' (Ibid., p. 17). The key here is correlation not, repeat not, a causation running from the real wage to employment. He continues his argument: 'Thus if employment increases, then, in the short period, the reward per unit of labour in terms of wage-goods must, in general, decline and profits increase' (Ibid., p. 17). And again he reiterates, 'any means of increasing employment must lead at the same time to a diminution of the marginal product and hence of the rate of wages measured in terms of this product' (Ibid., p. 18). The causal sequence is absolutely clear; it is from employment to the real wage. The determinant of employment, given supply conditions, is given by effective demand: 'The amount of labour which the entrepreneurs decide to employ depends on the sum [D] of two quantities, namely D_1, the amount which the community is expected to spend on consumption, and D_2, the amount which it is expected to devote to new investment. D is what we have called ... effective demand' (Ibid., p. 29).

We have shown that the term involuntary unemployment was in use well before Keynes brought it to the fore. We have also presented evidence for our earlier assertion that involuntary unemployment was part and parcel of Keynes's new effective demand theory of employment. He did discuss it in a manner that could and did lead to a complete distortion of his intended meaning. Perhaps he should not have used the term – as we have seen it had been used well before his contribution in a very different sense so perhaps there was bound to be confusion. Words used in economics are rarely ethically neutral and as we have argued it may well be that *Keynes used the term intentionally to take the blame for mass unemployment away from labour – organized or not – and on to the economic system itself.*

But the orthodox interpretation of Keynes did not accept this interpretation, rather, be it in its neo-classical synthesis form, its monetarist form, or its new Keynesian form, the perfectionist hypothesis triumphed. The perfectionists see the perfect working of competitive markets as the optimum social arrangement and imperfections as leading to sub-optimal positions.[29] Unemployment is thus due to imperfections, i.e. wage stickiness. Thus we can either accept the resultant unemployment as voluntary – because the imperfections may arise from individual maximizing behaviour – or try supply-side measures to reduce it. Policy-wise we are back to labour supply. The discussion of policy measures to deal with unemployment have mirrored this discussion of blame. To this issue we now turn.

WHAT'S TO BE DONE – IF ANYTHING?

As an overview, the plain fact of the matter is the simple reply 'nothing much'. Positive action has amounted to trying to increase wage price flexibility and alter the trade-off between work and leisure so that the unemployed are encouraged back into work. With one or two exceptions there has always been support for the relief of distress and poverty that unemployment brings. Relief of the able-bodied poor was deemed to be necessary on humanitarian grounds or as often on the utilitarian grounds that the unemployed might revolt and overthrow the established order. McCulloch (quoted in O'Brien, 1970, p. 326 fn 8) said:

> although, therefore, the general principle as to self-reliance be as stated ... the economist or the politician who should propose carrying it out to its full extent in all cases and in all hazards, would be fitter for bedlam than for the closet or the cabinet. When any great number of work-people are thrown out of employment, they must be provided for by extraneous assistance in one way or another.

Fear of giving too much relief has been a common theme in the economics literature. This has been based on a multitude of beliefs but they all boil down to the incentives to undertake paid work. Perhaps derived from well-established fact (or rather the received wisdom!), economists have always operated on the assumption that workers, at least from the lower stratum of society, will up and depart from paid work at the drop of a hat. In the 19th century, the view of incentives was also combined with Malthusian fears that relief would sprout children who would rapidly join the ranks of the undeserving poor. Take this example from General Walker (1888, p. 358):

> why is it that the labourer works at all? Clearly that he may eat. If he may eat without it, he will not work. The neglect or contempt of this very obvious truth by the British Parliament, during the latter part of the eighteenth and early nineteenth century, brought the working classes of the kingdom almost to the verge of ruin, created a vast body of hopeless and hereditary pauperism, and engendered vices in the industrial system which has been productive of evil down to the present day.

Or from Beveridge about the voluntarily idle who should be 'removed from free industry and maintained adequately in public institutions, but with the complete and permanent loss of all civilian rights including not only the franchise but civil freedom and fatherhood'.

Similar, if not so explicitly extreme, views are prevalent today. Among the policy recommendations of an influential book on unemployment we read that we must 'take a tougher line on benefits' and that 'benefits can be made less attractive by cutting their value, by reducing their duration and by stiffening the work test' (Layard, Nickell and Jackman, 1991, p. 472). So basically economists have, as today, recommended supply-side policies to ameliorate unemployment. Reduce wages, reduce benefits, reduce the period of benefit eligibility, reduce public housing and other inhibitors to labour mobility. The cry has been reduction!

What of the other approach? The use of public employment as a policy weapon. The possibility that direct or indirect public employment projects (public works) might be used to ease unemployment has a long and respectable pedigree. We can, at least, start with Petty's famous suggestion that the unemployed 'be employed to build a useless pyramid upon Salisbury Plain, bring the stones at Stonehenge to Tower Hill, or the like' (quoted in Hutchison, 1988, p. 32). Suggestions continue in the 18th century (Sir James Steuart is but one example[30]), and in the 19th century we have quite a burst in the post-1815 period, much of it connected with Ireland.[31] At this stage there is not really a clear distinction between several issues that were to come to the fore in subsequent discussion. The salient points in the development of this topic were:

1. The distinction between relief work and public works. The distinction is blurred but basically relief was thought of as *ad hoc* arrangements consisting, for example, of subsidies to private production or local schemes funded by boards of guardians or charities. Public works were to be part of a planned development of the economy's, local or national, infrastructure. The emphasis here was on public employment.
2. The use of public works and the consequent public employment as part of a counter-cyclical programme to mop up cyclical unemployment and in the framework of a neutral full employment budget.
3. The use of public works and employment as part of a secular social capital strategy. This development relies on economic arguments about long-term demand deficient unemployment, or market failure theory.[32]

It is on point 2 that most economic discussion in the past has centred. What may be termed the technical discussion of the matter begins, as we have seen with other aspects of the unemployment literature, in the last quarter of the 19th century. In 1886 Foxwell writes: 'It is open to [the authorities] by a judicious distribution of public works, according to the condition of the labour market, to do much to balance the fluctuations of employment' (p. 255). A similar point was made by Dearle (1898), but the most famous early statement came in the first decade of the 20th century by the Webbs in the 1909 *Minority Report of the Poor Law Commission*. Beveridge (1910) gave conditional support and Pigou strongly defended counter-cyclical public works in his *Wealth of Welfare* (1912) and his *Unemployment* (1913). It is interesting to note that there was at this juncture no great opposition to these ideas via the so-called Treasury view. But undoubtedly the great impetus to the public works–public employment movement came with the theory of the multiplier as stated by Kahn and elaborated by Keynes in his *General Theory*. The multiplier appeared to answer the question 'where will the funds come from' to finance the public work schemes, and hence answer the 'Treasury view'.[33] I suppose the high point of the use of public works as a cyclical control weapon came towards the end of World War II and in the immediate post-war literature when the welter of books and reports on full employment all had a section on them. In the UK, for example, there was the 1944 White

Paper,[34] Beveridge's *Full Employment in a Free Society* (1944) and the Oxford Institute of Statistics, *Economics of Full Employment* (1944).

This advocacy of public employment as an integral part of unemployment amelioration did not last long. Economists soon shifted ground to the use of some mix of tax changes and monetary policy as control weapons. This shift has continued unabated until the present. The causes of it are complex but must include:

1. The greater acceptability to the business community of tax changes and monetary policy rather than direct public expenditures. This was especially so in the USA.
2. The realization that, as counter-cyclical devices, public employment schemes were not useful for 'fine tuning' in a model of built-in stabilization.[35]
3. The general denial of trade-off between unemployment and inflation, at least in the long run, and the acceptance of some version of the natural rate or NAIRU took demand-management, and hence the use of public employment, out of the realms of unemployment policy. We are left again, paralleling the discussion of causes with supply of labour-side policies to reduce unemployment. Policies have to be designed to help people find jobs. Jobs should not, indeed cannot, be found for them. So we are really back now in the immediate pre-Keynesian era as some commentators, for example Casson (1983), have observed.

CONCLUSION

The analyses of causes of and possible policies to reduce unemployment has been of recurring concern to economists, but it has not consistently held centre stage. In the perfectionalists' world that much of economic thought has dwelt in, job rationing – implying wage inflexibility – must be based on some maximizing strategy. Therefore, policies have concentrated on changing the characteristics of those without work to have greater incentives to find their place in the demand for labour. The alternative strategy of altering the structure of demand for labour to place people without work in jobs has only briefly surfaced. Like its allied concept of full employment, it has all but disappeared from the economists' vocabulary.

The salad days when it was mainstream to talk of the theory of full employment, and moreover to observe its actuality in the major industrial market economies, now seem to be over and that Keynesian episode is increasingly regarded as a freak situation to be studied by historians. One suspects though, and fervently hopes, that as high unemployment remains a feature of the world economy, economists will again turn their attention to the obvious facts of economic life. Our survey of economic thought and unemployment gives a glimmer of hope for the future.

NOTES

1. We should also remember Edwin Cannan's dictum that 'those who care for such trifling matters recognize three degrees of precedence in respect of the formulation of new economic doctrine. First, there is the discoverer; second, the anticipator of the discoverer; and third, the discoverer of the anticipator of the discoverer.' (Cannan, 1897).
2. I have in mind an economy where the norm is not a labour force consisting of full-time workers with a fixed working week. Some commentators argue that the post-industrial economy is a flexitime one.
3. In terms of modern unemployment analysis it is clear that the attempt to use mismatch between vacancies and unemployment as a measure of structural unemployment is full of difficulties once we notice that mismatch itself is correlated with the cycle.
4. Descriptions of the lives of the unemployed, the effects on them, and their families, both physically and mentally, on social discontent, crime and so on, are by and large now left to the sociological inquirer, unlike, for example, the late 19th-century studies where social and economic facts were happily intertwined. This just may be the inevitable consequence of the division of labour in social inquiry.
5. For an excellent discussion of the main issues involved in this controversy, see Hutchison (1988), chapter 8, appendix.
6. Allegations that a rise in the real wages would reduce the supply of labour, e.g. hours worked per week, predict a negative correlation between the real wage and employment in exactly the same manner as classical and neo-classical theories of the demand for labour!
7. This particular controversy is the subject of Chapter 2 of this volume.
8. Our remarks here refer to the UK, but growing unemployment, or rather a realization of its extent and social effects, also appears in the American literature. Writing on the question of the unemployed in Massachusetts, John Graham Brooks (1897) wrote: 'Discontent never got such a sharp and varied expression. Class hatreds never showed themselves in more sinister form. Socialist opinions were never before so widely uttered, nor have they at any time received in the press such universal attention.'
9. This is one of the earliest examples of commercial sponsorship of economic research. The prize was 'for the best essay on the present depression of trade'. See the preface to Alfred Russel Wallace's *Bad Times* (1885). Wallace's essay did not win!
10. At the height of the Keynesian era there was practically no opposition to his theoretical framework. Even erstwhile Austrians like Robbins (1947) confessed the error of their ways, as had Pigou (1945) who had been the prime object of attack in the *General Theory* (1936). A few Austrians, like Hayek, Hutt and Lachmann, did remain unrepentant.
11. There were some early warnings about the political feasibility of a full employment policy. Perhaps the most famous one was by Kalecki (1943, 1972).
12. In the USA, the tide had already turned against government spending by the early 1940s (see Collins (1981)).
13. The term is McCloskey's (1994): 'Young upwardly mobile indoctrinated economist always votes at his party's call, and never thinks of thinking for himself at all'.
14. The problem of gender and the history of economic thought more generally is raised in the mini symposium in the *History of Political Economy*, 25, 1993.
15. For the UK, Garside (1980) for example, warns against any estimates before 1850 and expresses grave reservations about any figures before the introduction of semi-comprehensive unemployment insurance in 1922.
16. The advocacy of differing macroeconomic policies seems to follow closely the swings in

political opinion. What is cause and what is effect is a matter of some controversy (see Corry (1995)).

17. It is not without a touch of irony that rigidities are central to the 'New' Keynesian economics, yet Keynes himself strongly denied that rigidities were essential to his theoretical construct.

18. Especially important in this development were the contributions of Lipsey (1960) and Samuelson and Solow (1960).

19. Evidence from Germany also suggests that before 1918 unemployment averaged about 3 per cent (Stachura, 1986, ch.1).

20. For example, Layard, Nickell and Jackman (1991, p. 41), in their influential study ('The green Bible'), write 'whether unemployment is voluntary or involuntary. The question is fruitless'.

21. As perhaps a rather extreme example of assumptions about unemployed people's characteristics, Charles Booth (1902, 1969, pp. 149–50) wrote, 'The unemployed are, as a class, a selection of the unfit, and, on the whole, those most in want are the most unfit'.

22. More exactly, the Labour Force Survey (LFS) definition of unemployment 'refers to people without a job who were available to start work in the two weeks following their LFS interview and had either looked for works in the four weeks prior to interview or were waiting to start a job they had already obtained' (*Labour Force Survey*, Historical Supplement, April 1993, p. 18).

23. See, for example, Carlin and Soskice (1990, p. 123).

24. On all of this see Howson and Winch (1977).

25. On this point, see Coddington (1983, ch. 3). Commentators have observed that even in the height of depression, unemployed workers blamed themselves for their situation. As Studs Terkel (quoted in Sherman, 1976, p. 6) writes: 'The suddenly idle hands blamed themselves, rather than society. True, there were hunger marches and protestations to City Hall and Washington, but the millions experienced a private kind of shame when the pink slips came. No matter that others suffered the same fate, the inner voice whispered, "I'm a failure".'

26. The use of the term 'equilibrium' in points 2 to 4 is deliberate. Whether analytically coherent or not – a matter much disputed in current discussions of Keynesian economics – Keynes himself always emphasized the equilibrium nature of his conclusions about the determination of the level of unemployment.

27. It is perhaps tempting to see in these quotations early versions of the natural rate or NAIRU hypotheses. But this temptation should be avoided. The two latter have no reference to any notion of full employment. The term is expunged from their vocabulary.

28. This interpretation is what we referred to earlier above as the perfectionist doctrine. See Eatwell and Milgate (1983).

29. Or, rather more subtly, the imperfections themselves are derived from optimizing behaviour on the part of employers (efficiency wage theory) or employees (insider–outsider theory).

30. See, for example, Eltis (1986).

31. See Black (1960, ch. 6).

32. Incidently I would place Keynes as much in the discussion of point (3) as (2).

33. The so-called 'Treasury view', implying complete crowding out of private employment by public employment, was not new of course. It has a long history going back to at least Ricardo and has been restated practically every generation. Take the following from Bastable (1917, p. 145: 'Some popular arguments for state expenditure may be at once dismissed. Perhaps the crudest is that which regards the State as affording employment.' On the Treasury view in the interwar period, see Peden (1984) and chapter 4 of this volume.

34. HMSO, Cmnd 6527, 1944.

35. The 'rules versus discretionary action' debate, initiated primarily by Friedman (1960) was a powerful weapon in the anti-public works campaign.

REFERENCES

Bastable, C.F. (1917), *Public Finance* (3rd edn) London: Macmillan & Co.

Berkeley, G. (1735, 1891), *The Querist*, in A.C. Fraser (ed.), *The Works of George Berkeley*, vol. 4, Oxford: Clarendon Press.

Beveridge, W. (1910), *Unemployment: A Problem of Industry*, London: Longmans.

Beveridge, W. (1944), *Full Employment in a Free Society*, London: Allen and Unwin.

Black, R.D.C. (1960), *Economic Thought and the Irish Question 1817–1870*, Cambridge: Cambridge University Press.

Booth, C. (1902, 1969), *Life and Labour of the People in London*, vol. 1, New York: Augustus Kelley.

Britton, A.J. (1994), *National Institute of Economic and Social Research Review*, November, 67.

Brooks, J.G. (1897), 'The question of the unemployed in Massachusetts', *Economic Journal*, 7, 361.

Brown, A.J. (1955), *The Great Inflation 1939–51*, London: Oxford University Press.

Cannan, E. (1897), 'What is capital?', *Economic Journal*, 7, 278.

Carlin, W. and Soskice, D. (1990), *Macroeconomics and the Wage Bargain*, Oxford: Oxford University Press.

Casson, M. (1983), *The Economics of Unemployment*, Oxford: Martin Robertson.

Clarke, P. (1988), *The Keynesian Revolution in the Making, 1924–1936*, Oxford: Clarendon Press.

Coddington, A. (1983), *Keynesian Economics: The Search for First Principles*, London: George Allen and Unwin.

Coleman, D. (1977), *The Economy of England 1458–1750*, Oxford: Oxford University Press.

Collins, R.M. (1981), *The Business Response to Keynes 1929–1964*, New York: Columbia University Press.

Corry, B.A. (1962), *Money, Saving and Investment in English Economics 1800–1850*, London: Macmillan & Co.

Corry, B.A. (1995), 'Politics and the Natural Rate Hypothesis: A Historical Perspective' in R. Cross (ed.), *The Natural Rate of Unemployment*, Cambridge: Cambridge University Press.

Dearle, N. (1898), *Problems of Unemployment in the London Building Trades*, London.

Eatwell, J. and Milgate, M. (1983), 'Unemployment and the Market Mechanism', in J. Eatwell and M. Milgate (eds), *Keynes's Economics and the Theory of Value and Distribution*, London: Duckworth.

Eltis, W. (1986), 'Sir James Steuart's Corporate State', in R.D.C. Black (ed.), *Ideas in Economics*, London: Macmillan Press.

Fawcett, Henry (1863), *Manual of Political Economy*, London: Macmillan & Co.

Fisher, I. (1926), 'A statistical relationship between unemployment and price changes', *International Labour Review*, June, 785–92.

Foxwell, H.S. (1886), 'Irregularities of Employment and Fluctuations of Prices', in J. Burnett (ed.), *The Claims of Labour*, Edinburgh: The Cooperative Printing.

Friedman, M. (1960), *A Program for Monetary Stability*, New York: Fordham University Press.

Garraty, J.A. (1978), *Unemployment in History. Economic Thought and Public Policy*, New York: Harper Row.

Garside, W.R. (1980), *The Measurement of Unemployment. Methods and Sources in Great Britain 1850–1979*, Oxford: Basil Blackwell.

Goodwin, L. (1972), *Do the Poor Want to Work?*, Washington: Brookings Institute.

Harris, J. (1972), *Unemployment and Politics. A Study in English Social Policy 1886–1914*, Oxford: Clarendon Press.

Harris, J. (1977), *William Beveridge: A Biography*, Oxford: Clarendon Press.

Hawtrey, R.G. (1913), *good and Bad Trade: An Analysis into the Causes of Trade Fluctuations*, London: Constable & Co.

Hobson, J.A. (1895), 'The meaning and measurement of unemployment', *The Contemporary Review*, **47**, March, 744–60.

Howson, S. and Winch, D. (1977), *The Economic Advisory Council 1930–39*, Cambridge: Cambridge University Press.

Hutchison, T.W. (1988), *Before Adam Smith. The Emergence of Political Economy 1662–1776*, Oxford: Basil Blackwell.

Kaldor, N. (1960), *Essays on Economic Stability and Growth*, London: G. Duckworth & Co.

Kalecki, M. (1943, 1972), 'Political aspects of full employment', *Political Quarterly*, **14**. Reprinted in E.K. Hunt and J.G. Schwartz (eds), *A Critique of Economic Theory*, Harmondsworth: Penguin Books.

Keynes, J.M. (1913, 1973), *Collected Writings*, vol. 13, 'Paper to the Political Economy Club', London: Macmillan.

Keynes, J.M. (1923, 1971), *Collected Writings*, vol. 4, *A Tract on Monetary Reform*, London: Macmillan.

Keynes, J.M. (1930, 1971), *Collected Writings*, vols 5 and 6, *A Treatise on Money*, London: Macmillan.

Keynes, J.M. (1936, 1973), *Collected Writings*, vol. 7, *The General Theory of Employment, Interest and Money*, London: Macmillan.

Keynes, J.M. (1971–89), *The Collected Writings of John Maynard Keynes*, London: Macmillan, for the Royal Economic Society.

Layard, R., Nickell, S. and Jackman, R. (1991), *Unemployment, Macroeconomic Performance and the Labour Market*, Oxford: Oxford University Press.

Lipsey, R.G. (1960), 'The relationship between unemployment and the rate of change of money wage rates in the UK 1862–1957', *Economica*, **27**, February, 456–87.

McCluskey, D. (1994), *Knowledge and Persuasion in Economics*, London: Cambridge University Press.

Marshall, A. (1923, 1965), *Money, Credit and Commerce*, New York: Augustus Kelley.

Marx, K. (1867, 1976), *Capital*, vol. 1, Harmondsworth, Penguin Books.

Mill, J.S. (1848, 1966), 'Principles of Political Economy' in J. Robson (ed.), *Collected Works of John Stuart Mill*, Toronto: University of Toronto Press (Routledge & Kegan Paul, vols 2 and 3).

O'Brien, D.P. (1970), *J.R. McCulloch. A Study in Classical Economics*, London: George Allen & Unwin.

Oxford Institute of Statistics (1994), *The Economics of Full Employment*, Oxford: Basil Blackwell.

Patinkin, D. (1982), *Anticipations of the General Theory*, London: Basil Blackwell.

Peden, G.C. (1984), 'The "Treasury View" on public works and employment in the inter-war period', *Economic History Review*, **37**, May, 167–81.

Phillips, A.W.H. (1958), 'The relationship between unemployment and the rate of change of money wage rates in the United Kingdom 1861–1979', *Economica*, **25**, November, 283–99.

Pigou, A.C. (1912), *Wealth and Welfare*, London: Macmillan & Co.

Pigou, A.C. (1913), *Unemployment*, London: Williams & Norgate, Home University of Modern Knowledge.

Pigou, A.C. (1945), *Lapses from Full Employment*, London: Macmillan & Co.

Pribram, K. (1935), 'Unemployment', in E.R.A. Seligman and A. Johnson (eds), *Encyclopaedia of Social Sciences*, New York: The Macmillan Co.

Ricardo, D. (1821, 1951–55), *The Works and Correspondence of David Ricardo*, edited by P. Sraffa with the collaboration of M.H. Dobb, vol. 1, Cambridge: Cambridge University Press.

Robbins, L.C. (1947), *The Economic Problem in Peace and War*, London: Macmillan & Co.

Robertson, D.H. (1915, 1948), *A Study of Industrial Fluctuation*, London: London School of Economics (series of reprints of scarce works on political economy, 8).

Rowntree, B.S. (1901), *Poverty: A Study of Town Life*, London: Macmillan & Co.

Rymes, T.K. (1989), *Keynes Lectures 1932–35*, London: Macmillan.

Samuelson, P.A. and Solow, R. (1960), 'Analytic aspects of anti-inflation policy', *American Economic Review*, **50**, 177–94.

Sherman, H.J. (1976), *Stagflation: A Radical Theory of Unemployment and Inflation*, New York: Harper & Row.

Southall, H.R. (1988), 'The origins of the depressed areas', *Economic History Review*, **41** (2), 236–58.

Stachura, P.D. (ed.) (1986), *Unemployment and the Great Depression in Weimar Germany*, London: Macmillan & Co.

Vickers, D. (1960), *Studies in the Theory of Money 1690–1776*, London: Peter Owen.

Walker, F.A. (1888), *Political Economy*, New York: Macmillan & Co.

Wallace, A.R. (1885), *Bad Times*, London: Macmillan & Co.

Webb, S. and Webb, B. (1911), *The Prevention of Destitution*, London: Longmans Green & Co. (This volume contains most of the minority report.)

Webb, S. and Webb, B. (1929), *English Poor Law History, Part 2: The Last Hundred Years*, London: Longmans Green & Co.

2. Ricardo and Malthus on the post-Napoleonic distress: too many producers or a momentary lapse of reason?*

Terry Peach

INTRODUCTION

The period following the defeat of Napoleon in 1815 was one of acute economic turbulence in Britain. There was, it seems, a general sense of shock and bewilderment at the scale of the 'distress', as it was called, that came to afflict agriculture, manufacturing and commerce. And, as levels of unemployment soared, so the demands for government to do *something* rose to a crescendo. The reactions of Ricardo and Malthus to the train of post-war events provide two contrasting perspectives on what could, or should, be done. In Ricardo's case, the 'true' principles of political economy led him to the somewhat counterfactual position that the distress ought not even be happening, certainly not on the scale, nor for the duration, that was actually being experienced. To the extent that he could make any sense of it at all, its severity was attributed to blind irrationality on the part of the capitalist class. As to the scope for remedial government intervention, he held steadfastly to the position that the only helpful policies would be the repayment of the national debt and, over the longer term, the deregulation of trade, especially in corn. Moreover, as far as he was concerned it was, or rather it should be, the responsibility of the labouring classes themselves both to regulate their number to the demand for labour and to provide a contingency fund to tide them over any spells of short-term unemployment. Tackling unemployment directly was not the business of government.

*Previous versions of this chapter were presented to the UK Spring History of Economic Thought Conference, Gresham College, London; to the Department of Economics, University of Amsterdam; and to the 1995 US History of Economics Society Conference, University of Notre Dame, Indiana. I am particularly grateful to A. Dutt (University of Notre Dame) and J. Salter (University of Manchester) who may have prevented at least one momentary lapse of reason on my part. Lapses remaining are, I am afraid, entirely my own responsibility.

Malthus took a different view. Although he shared Ricardo's belief that the onus of responsibility should ultimately fall on the labouring population to adjust itself to the demand for labour without government intervention, he did not share Ricardo's conviction that capital accumulation and an accompanying increasing demand for labour would *necessarily* be forthcoming to reduce unemployment from the demand side. On the contrary, his analysis of Britain's economic distress eventually led him to the conclusion that unemployment would persist and that if events were left to unfold under their own dynamic, the level of unemployment was more likely to rise than to fall. This in turn raised a problem which for Ricardo was non-existent: what could, or should, be done for the unemployed in such dire circumstances? According to the interpretation that I challenge in this chapter, Malthus's answer was to boost demand by means of a public works programme, so restoring economic activity directly *by acting upon demand conditions.*[1]

The interpretation of Malthus as a 'demand-manager' may appear quite plausible. If, as he undoubtedly contended, the pervasive economic problem was one of a deficient level of demand relative to supply, and if, as he also contended, a large measure of 'unproductive consumption' was required even under normal conditions to ensure an adequate level of demand, then the diversion of funds to support labourers in unproductive, government-directed occupations may naturally suggest itself as a policy of demand expansion. Yet such a rationale was not advanced by Malthus himself. On the contrary, to the extent that the 'mature' Malthus explicitly advanced any strictly economic argument in favour of public works, it was that capital would be thereby diverted from existing employments, thus tending to reduce *supply* which would therefore create (no more than) the pre-conditions for future growth. Yet it is arguable that Malthus was theoretically equipped to advocate a policy of demand-management had he been so minded. I suggest, however, that there are compelling reasons to believe that Malthus would not have wished to support a more active policy of government intervention.

In the following sections I explore in turn the positions of Ricardo and Malthus. Greater attention will be paid to Malthus, partly because I have presented my interpretation of Ricardo elsewhere,[2] but also because Malthus's position is, I think, the more interesting one.

RICARDO ON THE DISTRESS

Writing to Malthus on hearing the news of Napoleon's defeat, Ricardo declared himself in no doubt that the country could look forward to 'a long period of prosperity' (27 June 1815, *R Works*, VI, p. 232[3]). The theoretical support for his optimism came from the doctrine known as the 'Law of Markets'.

Put simply, Ricardo's version of the 'Law' can be reduced to two general propositions. First, on the consumption side, Ricardo presumed that each individual's desire to consume *something* other than food was limited only by income.[4] Second, on the supply side, it was presumed that capitalists (nearly) always can and will find something to produce which will yield them at least the going general rate of profit on their investment, the only qualification being that they will cease to produce if general profitability does not cover basic risks. Thus, all income will be spent on commodities which tend to exchange at their 'natural prices',[5] with the monetary value of national income always *tending* to equality with the monetary value of national output.[6] Moreover, capital will continue to accumulate indefinitely providing only that general profitability is above the minimum level. It should also be noted that the only basis for a 'permanent' reduction in general profitability according to Ricardo was a worsening in the conditions of producing the wage-goods entering the 'natural' wage-bundle.[7]

Ricardo's reaction to the events of the post-Napoleonic period may be considered in the light of the above model. The first major shock to the economic system came from a glut of corn in 1815 which resulted in a fall in agricultural profitability, in rents and in agricultural employment. Ricardo conceded that the agricultural distress was unfortunate for those involved, but it did not, or rather it should not, imply a more general malaise. On the contrary, according to his theoretical perspective a lower corn price *should* be followed by lower money wages, higher profitability in manufacturing and therefore *increased* economic activity as capitalists expand their output in consequence of their greater 'power' to accumulate from enhanced profits. Nor would the reduction in the incomes of farmers and landlords present an obstacle to expansion. Capitalists could either produce more commodities to satisfy the unlimited desires of each other or, in the worst case (considered highly improbable by Ricardo), they could forgo their own immediate consumption and produce consumption goods to satisfy the unlimited desires of their workers (although this would have the effect of reducing profitability prior to a wage-induced population expansion).

As events unfolded it became clear that the economy was not behaving according to Ricardo's theoretical vision. During 1816 the continuing agricultural distress was accompanied by a declining demand for British exports and pervasive distress in manufacturing.[8] Against the background of rising unemployment, 'bread and blood' riots and episodes of frame-breaking, Ricardo wrote to his friend Hutches Trower:

Surely the disastrous effects which always attend an important change in the employments of capital cannot much longer continue and we shall soon witness a renovation of commercial activity and credit. (15 July 1816, *R Works*, VII, p. 49)

Outside agriculture, the problem was viewed by Ricardo as the merely frictional one of reallocating capital (and labour) to peace-time occupations. As for agriculture itself, Ricardo advanced the remarkable suggestion that landlords 'ought to rejoice in the evidence which the low price of produce affords of the yet unexhausted state of the resources of the country' (letter to Trower, 4 February 1816, *R Works*, VII, p. 16). But Ricardo's hopes of an imminent return to economic prosperity were to prove unfounded. The general distress continued during the first few months of 1817, with a rate of unemployment estimated by one contemporary observer at approaching 30 per cent of the labouring population.[9] Commenting on a proposal to employ labourers on public works, Ricardo wrote to Malthus:

> I am not one of those who think that the raising of funds for the purpose of employing the poor is a very efficacious mode of relief, as it diverts those funds from other employments which would be equally if not more productive to the community. That part of the capital which employs the poor on the roads for example cannot fail to employ men somewhere and I believe every interference is prejudicial. (To Malthus, 3 January 1817, *R Works*, VII, p. 116)

This was not particularly convincing, since it must have been apparent to most contemporary observers that capital was *not* being employed productively. But it does serve to underline Ricardo's conviction that there was no *active*, interventionist role for government to play in stimulating economic activity.

As the months of 1817 passed it seemed to Ricardo that, not before time, his hopes for a revival were being realized, at least in manufacturing. He wrote confidently to Malthus:

> I doubt whether we have even during the late distress ceased to advance as a nation in wealth, but at present I think no one can doubt that we are again making forward strides in prosperity. (To Malthus, 4 September 1817, *R Works*, VII, pp. 185–6)

But, once again, his hopes were to be dashed. By March of 1819 the economic picture had returned to one of gloom, gluts, stagnation, unemployment and riots. Ricardo corresponded:

> We all have to lament the present distressed situation of the labouring classes in this country, but the remedy is not very apparent to me. (To Brown, 13 October 1819, *R Works*, VIII, p. 103)

Indeed it was not. For the longer term, Ricardo believed that a movement towards free trade would increase opportunities for investment, growth and employment; and he also briefly sang along to the popular Whig tune that the burden of the national debt and high levels of taxation were responsible for a 'deficiency' of capital and hence for unemployment;[10] according to his model, returned taxes would necessarily increase the aggregate demand for consumption and production goods and this would (or should) be met by a corresponding increase in supply and in levels of employment. But none of those factors could explain why the employment of the *existing* capital stock was attended with such disastrous consequences: consequences that ran directly counter to the 'Law of Markets' doctrine.

The only explanation left to Ricardo was the misallocation of capital: capitalists were producing the wrong things. Yet such perverse behaviour was only supposed to continue 'for no more than one or two years' (to Trower, 26 September 1820, *R Works*, VIII, p. 257) and it had taken unforeseen events to wring even that concession out of Ricardo. His sense of bewilderment, and his exasperation at the seemingly irrational behaviour of capitalists, is conveyed by the following extract from a well-known letter to Malthus:

> Men err in their productions, there is no deficiency of demand. If I wanted cloth, and you cotton goods, it would be great folly in us both with a view to an exchange between us, for one of us to produce velvets and the other wine, – we are guilty of some such folly now, and I can scarcely account for the length of time that this delusion continues. (9 October 1820, *R Works*, VIII, pp. 277–8.)

MALTHUS ON THE DISTRESS

Malthus's most developed account of the post-war economic distress – including his analysis of its genesis and his fullest discussion of possible measures to alleviate its effects – is contained in his *Principles* of 1820.[11] His earlier position(s) do, however, merit preliminary consideration.

Malthus's 'mature' analysis of Britain's economic difficulties was to some extent anticipated in earlier correspondence with Ricardo in which Malthus challenged the legitimacy of the 'Law of Markets'. Thus, during the latter half of 1814, Malthus argued that those who possess revenue will *not* necessarily wish to consume to the full extent of their 'power'; that the expenditure of unspent consumption balances on investment will *not* provide a solution to the problem of an insufficiency of 'effectual demand';[12] that the constraint on the growth of rich countries is the inherent difficulty of inspiring new 'wants and tastes' in (rich) consumers; and that consequently there must exist the *potential* for a reduction in general profitability owing to a deficiency in 'effectual demand' relative to the aggregate supply of commodities (the general glut thesis).[13] None of these propositions met with Ricardo's assent. Malthus also canvassed a possible scenario which was later to acquire greater significance:

Accumulation of *produce* is not accumulation of *capital*, unless what is accumulated is worth more than it cost, and if you were at once to employ all our soldiers sailors and menial servants in productive labour, the price of produce would fall more than ten per cent, and the encouragement to employ the same quantity of capital would cease. (To Ricardo, 23 November 1814, *R Works*, VI, p. 155, original emphasis)[14]

By implication, a certain amount of *unproductive* consumption (in the above context, the consumption of soldiers, sailors and menial servants, who do not themselves produce material output) may be necessary to sustain an adequate level of (aggregate) effectual demand: an argument developed in Malthus's *Principles* of 1820.

The revision of his *Essay on the Principle of Population* (hereafter abbreviated to *Essay*) for a fifth edition, published in 1817, provided Malthus with a formal opportunity to state his evolving thoughts on Britain's economic problems. His position in the *Essay* is interesting, not just in its own right but also, more importantly for my purposes, because it may shed light on the reasons for his later reticence on the issue of government intervention.

The distress and accompanying unemployment were attributed by Malthus to a deficiency in the level of effectual demand relative to output:

among the mercantile and manufacturing classes, where the greatest numbers are without employment, the evil obviously arises, not so much from the want of capital and the means of production, as the want of a market for the commodity when produced. (*M Works*, III, p. 379)

Yet, at this time at least, Malthus held out the hope (shared by Ricardo, if for somewhat different reasons[15]) that the distress was only temporary. Thus, he predicted that the economic situation, including employment prospects, *would* improve owing to a combination of a reduction in the net birth rate among labourers, 'the increasing wants of Europe and America from their increasing riches, and the adaptation of the supply of commodities at home to the new distribution of wealth occasioned by the alteration of the circulating medium' (*M Works*, III, p. 377). But, unlike Ricardo, this diagnosis of a temporary problem was not accompanied by recommendations either for total policy-inaction or for a reduction in levels of taxation and government debt.

The principal danger involved in extinguishing the national debt and in reducing levels of taxation (policies favoured by Ricardo) was, Malthus argued, that the associated reduction in the government-financed demand for manufactured output would not be matched immediately by the effectual demands of the beneficiaries, even under the most favourable circumstances: 'it would be a considerable time before the new wants and tastes of the enriched [persons] had restored the former demand', he opined (*M Works*, III, p. 378); but, worse still, Malthus thought it 'probable' that the (rich) beneficiaries were more likely to spend their additional income on 'horses, hounds and menial servants' than on produced commodities, with the result that 'the substituted demand would be very much less favourable to the increase of the capital and general resources of the country' (*M Works*, III, pp. 378–9). Thus, on the basis of a proposition fiercely contested by Ricardo – that an individual's demand for commodities of 'luxury and convenience' is *not* unlimited – Malthus contended that such government policies would only make matters worse.

But were there any government policies that might alleviate the (albeit temporary) problem? Malthus apparently thought there were not; or at least, he did not point to any policy that could make an *overall* difference to levels of economic activity and employment. Thus, he wrote, for example, that 'it is impracticable by any exertions, either individual *or national*, to restore at once that brisk demand for commodities and labour which has been lost by events, that, however they may have originated, *are now beyond the Power of control*' (*M Works*, III, p. 375, emphasis added). One would not immediately identify these sentiments as those of a proto-Keynesian interventionist.

At the same time, Malthus *did* endorse a public works programme of the sort which had been summarily dismissed by Ricardo. It 'would be desirable if possible', he wrote, 'to employ those that were out of work, if it were merely to avoid the bad moral effects of idleness, and of the evil habits which might be generated by depending for a considerable time on mere alms' (*M Works*, III, p. 376). He continued:

> But ... we ought to proceed ... with great caution, and ... the kinds of employment which ought to be chosen are those, the results of which will not interfere with existing capitals. Such are public works of all descriptions, the making and repairing of roads, bridges, railways, canals, etc.; and now, perhaps, since the great loss of agricultural capital, almost every sort of labour upon the land, which could be carried on by public subscription. (*M. Works*, III, p. 376)

Importantly, however, such measures were not advocated on the grounds of a resulting net increase in the level of unemployment. Thus:

> the benefit to some must bring with it disadvantages to others. That portion of each person's revenue which might go in subscriptions of this kind, must of course be lost to the various sorts of labour which its expenditure in the usual channels would have supported; and the want of demand thus occasioned in these channels must cause the pressure of distress to be felt in quarters which might otherwise have escaped it. But this is an effect which, in such cases, it is impossible to avoid. (*M Works*, III, pp. 376–7)

In other words, Malthus vintage 1817 did not disagree entirely with Ricardo's judgement 'that the raising of funds for the purpose of employing the poor is

[not] a very efficacious mode of relief, as it diverts those funds from other employments' (*R Works*, VII, p. 116): a shared position implying a presumed absence of unspent money balances or, in 'classical' parlance, the 'no hoarding' principle.

It follows that Malthus's programme of public works would save only *some* labourers from 'the bad moral effects of idleness' (etc.), while simultaneously inflicting those effects on others who would be thrown out of employment as a direct consequence of the self-same policy. The net outcome would merely be to spread the misery, as Malthus himself made clear:

> as a temporary measure, it is not only charitable but just, to spread the evil over a larger surface, in order that its violence on particular parts may be so mitigated as to be made bearable by all. (*M Works*, III, p. 377)

The position thus remains that government was apparently considered powerless to make a significant difference to the overall economic situation.

That the thesis of government impotence was not an unconsidered position of Malthus's at this time is supported by his comments on the *political* consequences of the distress. In Book IV, Chapter VII of the *Essay*, newly added to the 1817 edition, Malthus propounded the argument that the growing support for political reform among 'the lower classes' had been fuelled by a misapprehension both of the causes of their poverty and unemployment and of the possible solutions to their plight. Government, he argued, was *not* mainly responsible for the distress; nor was it in the power of *any* government, however constituted, to provide remedies for the causes of the distress: they (the causes) were 'to a certain extent and for a certain time, *irremediable*' (*M Works*, III, p. 512, emphasis added). Unfortunately (from Malthus's perspective) the labourers were too ignorant and deluded to grasp those economic realities and had allowed themselves to be duped 'by the popular orators and writers' who had 'raise[d] unreasonable and extravagant expectations as to the relief to be expected from reform' (*M Works*, III, p. 512). Malthus was plainly alarmed by the possible consequences:

> If under these circumstances the reforms proposed had been accomplished, it is impossible that the people should not have been most cruelly disappointed; and under a system of universal suffrage and annual parliaments, a general disappointment of the people would probably lead to every sort of experiment in government, till the career of change was stopped by a military despotism. The warmest friends of genuine liberty might justly feel alarmed at such a prospect. (*M Works*, III, p. 512)

But, of course, if government *did* have the power to combat the distress through demand-management, and was currently choosing not to exercise that power, the situation would be very different: the popular orators and writers might then have a rational basis for arguing that relief could be forthcoming only with a more democratically elected government. And as an opponent of the popular reform movement,[16] Malthus would have found himself in a distinctly uncomfortable position.

And so to Malthus's *Principles* of 1820. The focus of my discussion is on Malthus's analysis of the possible means of alleviating the distress and, particularly, his position on the scope and rationale for government intervention. First, however, I consider Malthus's account of the origins of the distress and various theoretical issues arising from it.

Malthus's diagnosis of Britain's economic ills proceeded as follows.[17] The economic crisis had been triggered by a glut of agricultural output which was immediately responsible for a fall in agricultural profitability, a fall in rents and the destruction of agricultural capital. In turn, the fall in rents and in agricultural profits resulted in a reduction in landlords' and farmers' demands for manufactured output which provoked a fall in manufacturing profitability and glutted domestic markets.[18] Manufacturers had responded by attempting to export their surpluses but in doing so they had succeeded only in glutting markets overseas. Unemployment thus increased as agriculture, manufacturing and foreign trade languished. At the same time, the (potential) labouring population was continuing to expand, partly as a lagged response to the relatively high wages which had prevailed during the war, but also because of the demobilization of the army and navy. The increase in unemployment had the *eventual* result of reducing both money and real (commodity) wages, but the result was not a rise in profits. Profits remained low, Malthus argued, owing to a deficiency in the effectual demand for output. Then, to compound the misery, returned taxes (or at least some of them) had been channelled into saving and investment, but this had served only to exacerbate the general problem of over-production relative to the effectual demand.[19] Barring a large but unlikely increase in effectual demand, and in the absence of government intervention, Malthus's account suggests that the market solution to the crisis would be the destruction (and emigration) of capital and a consequential reduction in national output and income to the point where the reduced supply of goods would yield 'acceptable' profits to capitalists. In this process of economic contraction, however, unemployment would continue to spiral ever higher.[20]

Several features of the above account deserve elaboration, particularly: the relationships envisaged by Malthus between wages, profits and accumulation; the importance of satiation; and the role Malthus ascribed to 'excessive' saving together with the associated matter of the saving-investment relationship.

In Ricardo's opinion, a reduction in wages would have the effect of *increasing* profits which would lead to more capital accumulation and therefore an increased demand for labour. For Malthus, however, movements in wages (nominal or 'real', the latter in the Smithian sense of the commodities that labourers can purchase) were only one factor governing profitability since, as Adam Smith had argued, the other, potentially *independent* influence was the relationship between the supply and the effectual demand for output.[21] Malthus believed that profits and wages had *both* fallen, the former owing to a deficiency of effectual demand relative to the supply. Such a situation was incomprehensible to Ricardo and, indeed, it is arguable that Malthus never succeeded in mounting a cogent argument to the contrary. But, even supposing that the reduction in wages had, to some extent, resulted in higher profits, Malthus's model, unlike Ricardo's, did not predict an automatic increase in accumulation; or, more accurately, it did not predict an automatic increase in 'effective' accumulation, i.e. accumulation that would not terminate in lower profitability. For, if the effectual demand for output had not increased, the attempt by capitalists to expand production would inevitably result in lower prices and profits and the destruction of capital. Thus, although it is true that Malthus regarded 'high' profits as a *necessary* condition for accumulation (because they gave the capitalists the 'power and the will' to accumulate), they were not sufficient to ensure *effective* accumulation. 'Effective', or sustainable, accumulation was a function of profit *and effectual demand*.

A second, major difference between Ricardo and Malthus concerns the role played by the satiation of desires.[22] To Ricardo, the situation presented by Malthus was absurd. It was empirically inconceivable to him that those in possession of the 'power' to consume would not exercise it to the utmost extent; from which it followed that the 'problem', if indeed it existed, was merely one of producing the 'wrong' commodities. But also, on the supposedly counterfactual assumption that satiation *was* the problem, Ricardo could see no reason why capitalists *would* continue to pursue the suicidal strategy of producing without a market.[23] To Ricardo, the argument thus appeared to rest on a presumed irrationality on the part of the capitalist class: an allegation that also bears on the crucial role ascribed by Malthus to 'excessive' saving.[24]

The question of whether, and to what extent, Malthus *did* explain the relative deficiency of effectual demand in terms of the conversion of *additional* savings into additional investment and output is a contentious one. Some commentators, including Samuel Hollander (1969), have claimed that such an explanation was not advanced by Malthus. Yet, if they are correct, one is surely at a loss to understand Malthus's claim that the distress had arisen 'from that disturbance in the balance of produce and consumption, which has been occasioned by the sudden conversion of soldiers, sailors, and various other classes which the war employed, *into productive labourers*' (*M Works*, VI, p. 342, emphasis added).[25] Furthermore, Malthus's concern over the effects of repaying the national debt (a policy favoured by Ricardo) turned precisely on the point that the resulting increase in savings-investment *would* aggravate the distress by increasing output relative to a flat level of effectual demand (*M Works*, VI, pp. 433).[26] It is therefore difficult to agree with the proposition that 'excessive' saving-investment played no part whatever in Malthus's analysis.

I therefore see little reason to question the associated interpretation that Malthus was at one with Ricardo in equating acts of saving with acts of investment.[27] But this raises a further question. With acts of saving equated with acts of investment, how could Malthus maintain (as he did) that the distress was caused by a deficiency of effectual demand relative to output? Ricardo could never understand the argument, and he is not alone in that respect. According to Corry (1959), for example, no such deduction is logically possible, which indeed it is not *within the textbook Keynesian framework*. For, if a decision to abstain from present consumption necessarily implies a corresponding decision to demand capital assets, one cannot deduce a reduction in aggregate demand from a reduction in consumption. In Malthus's framework, however, the position is rather different. It is true that Malthus recognized the existence of investment goods as distinct from capital invested in the direct 'support' of productive labour (labour involved in the production of material commodities), but Malthus's presumption appears to have been that saving-investment is to be viewed in terms of its 'ultimate' effect of increasing the output of *consumption goods*.[28] And, from that perspective, one may perhaps begin to understand, if not condone, Malthus's argument that increased saving-investment, and *therefore* increased output of consumption goods, must result in a fall in profitability in the absence of a greater effectual demand on the part of non-labourers. However, as Ricardo counter-argued repeatedly, Malthus's 'over-investment' scenario can always be translated as a case of profits falling because of rising (commodity) wages;[29] and, moreover, the process of over-investment may continue *providing* the rate of profit remains above its minimum level.[30] It may suffice to say that there was no meeting of minds between the two protagonists on the 'true cause' of the fall in profits.

I now turn to Malthus's discussion of the possible solutions, and non-solutions, to the distress. His belief that a reduction in taxation (and/or the extinction of the national debt) would only make matters worse has been noted above, the argument being that any resulting increase in savings-investment would merely accentuate the fundamental problem of general over-production relative to the effectual demand.[31] By the same reasoning, he also gave short shrift to the argument that exhortations to save more and spend less (on immediate consumption) could provide a remedy.[32] What, then, were the remaining options?

One possibility, at least in principle, would be to encourage an increase in the effectual demand for objects of luxury and convenience on the part of the 'higher and middle' classes. Indeed, of all the effectual demands, those for 'luxuries' were consistently held up by Malthus as the most important for stimulating growth.[33] More precisely, *increases* in such effectual demands were claimed to provide the 'temporary' high profits which Malthus lauded as the main and, because not accompanied by a reduction in the effectual demands of capitalists, the most desirable source for additional saving and accumulation.[34] Thus, all would be well if the effectual demand for luxuries could be increased. But the prospects for achieving this objective were not considered encouraging.

The general difficulty of inspiring new desires for luxuries – a fictitious difficulty, according to Ricardo – was described by Malthus thus:

> an efficient taste for luxuries, that is, such a taste as will properly stimulate industry, instead of being ready to appear at the moment it is required, is a plant of slow growth. (*M Works*, VI, p. 258)

The 'taste' is, it seems, something that develops very gradually and is reflected in, and also influenced by, the process of capital accumulation over time.[35] However, there was one policy that could, in principle, play an important part in stimulating new desires: the extension of foreign trade. The introduction of new, imported objects of desire could stimulate an otherwise torpid desire to increase consumption among the rich[36] while, at the same time, increased overseas demand for domestic output would furnish the temporary high profits out of which additional accumulation could be financed. But the most likely way of increasing foreign trade was through the removal of restrictions and to adopt such a policy would have the immediate effect of making matters worse (a point on which Ricardo and Malthus were agreed):

> Humanity may ... require that the freedom of trade should be restored only by slow gradations, and with a good degree of reserve and circumspection. Were ... high duties and prohibitions taken away all at once, cheaper foreign goods of the same kind might be poured so fast into the home market as to deprive all at once many thousands of their ordinary employment and means of subsistence. (*M Works*, VI, p. 341)

And so, at least in the circumstances of post-war Britain, there was nothing much that could be achieved on this particular front.

Another route to increasing the consumption of material luxuries would be to redistribute income from the super-rich to the moderately rich. This, Malthus argued, could be achieved by breaking up large landed estates; and because the moderately rich were presumed to have a greater preference than the super-rich for consuming material commodities rather than the services of (menial) unproductive labourers, the result would be an increase in the level of economic activity.[37] However, the landed aristocracy were also viewed by Malthus as the guardians of the unwritten British Constitution, which he had no wish to see imperilled. '[H]igher considerations … than those which relate to mere wealth' (*M Works*, VI, p. 303), i.e. the preservation of the political status quo, thus dictated that no action could be taken on this front either.

I turn to the prospects for stimulating effective demand by increasing the consumption of productive labourers. Although the demands of productive labourers were considered by Malthus as 'an important part' of the national demand for output[38] – they were 'effectual' in providing a demand for wage-goods, at least under normal circumstances – they could never be sufficient to encourage capital accumulation: 'nobody will ever employ capital merely for the sake of the demand occasioned by those whose work for him', Malthus declared flatly (*M Works*, VI, p. 322). As for the idea canvassed by Ricardo, that *if* the capitalists (and others) did not wish to consume output, production could be redirected to satisfying the (unlimited) material demands of the productive labourers themselves, Malthus argued that the reduction in profits implied by the strategy would lead to a reduction in accumulation: 'as a great increase of consumption among the working classes must greatly increase the cost of production, it must lower profits, and diminish or destroy the motive to accumulate' (*M Works*, VI, pp. 322–3). Thus, any attempt to compensate for the relatively deficient level of effectual demand by increasing the per capita incomes of productive labourers would prove to be disastrous (even assuming that it could be done).[39]

The only possibility remaining would be to increase effectual demand by increasing the incomes or number of unproductive labourers. It is well known that, much to Ricardo's horror, Malthus extolled the virtues of maintaining a body of unproductive consumers, including unproductive labourers, on the grounds not only of the useful public and private services that they performed but also because their consumption filled the gap that was otherwise likely to exist between the income and consumption of the rich.[40] It is, indeed, the linkage of this important (and indubitable) feature of Malthus's system with his reaffirmed endorsement of a programme of public works which seems to provide the most compelling argument in favour of Malthus's reputation as a demand-manager.

The passage from the *Principles* in which Malthus lent his support to a programme of public works merits lengthy quotation:

It is also of importance to know that, in our endeavours to assist the working classes in a period like the present, it is desirable to employ them in unproductive labour, or at least in labour, the results of which do not come for sale into the market, such as roads and public works. The objection to employing a large sum in this way, raised by taxes, would not be its tendency to diminish the capital employed in productive labour; because this, to a certain extent, is exactly what is wanted; but it might, perhaps, have the effect of concealing too much the failure of the national demand for labour, and prevent the population from gradually accommodating itself to a reduced demand. This however might be ... corrected by the wages given. And altogether I should say, that the employment of the poor in roads and public works, and a tendency among landlords and persons of property to build, to improve and beautify their grounds, and to employ workmen and menial servants, are the means most within our power and most directly calculated to remedy the evils arising from ... [the] disturbance in the balance of produce and consumption. (*M Works*, VI, p. 342)

Those who regard Malthus as a 'demand manager' are presumably crediting him with the belief that 'the employment of the poor in roads and public works' will increase the general level of effectual demand, employment and prosperity. There is a case that could be made along those lines. If at least some of the new public employees were previously unemployed, any resulting increase in the effectual demand for wage-goods would at least increase the profits of some capitalists and, perhaps, stimulate a combination of new capital accumulation, an increased demand for luxuries and a rise in the level of employment. But this case was not developed explicitly by Malthus himself. Indeed, an indication that Malthus was not envisaging a significant demand-induced increase in the level of economic activity is implied by his injunction that the labouring population *must* accommodate itself 'to a reduced demand'. What, then, was the economic rationale for public works?

The aim of the policy was to 'make the supply and consumption bear a more advantageous proportion to each other, so as to increase the exchangeable value of the whole produce' (*M Works*, VI, p. 342). But this objective can be secured either by increasing the aggregate effectual demand *or by decreasing supply*. And the latter was precisely the *explicit* effect that the taxation-financed public works programme would have; taxation would have the *desirable* consequence of diminishing 'the capital employed in productive labour' (implying a reduction in the supply of output). As Malthus wrote on the same theme in his *High and Low Prices* (1823):

Whenever, within certain limits, a portion of the produce of a country has been diminished, by the seasons, by obstructions to importation, *or by an increase in the proportion of unproductive consumption*, not only does the power of setting fresh industry in motion remain unimpaired, but by the universal law of the effect of quantity upon price it is greatly increased (*M Works*, VII, pp. 242–3, emphasis added)

I therefore suggest that a public works programme was endorsed by Malthus not so much because it would increase effectual demand *but because it would reduce supply*.

The interpretation of Malthus as a 'supply-manager' raises at least two intriguing questions. First, *could* Malthus have argued consistently with his general analysis that government intervention might provide a solution to the distress? And second, if his theoretical position *would* support a policy of demand management, why was the policy not articulated by him?

There are grounds for giving at least a qualified affirmative answer to the first question. If unproductive consumption is necessary under normal circumstances to sustain a certain level of productive activity, as Malthus maintained, it does not seem a gigantic leap to argue that an *increase* in unproductive consumption might call forth an increase in such activity.[41] And, indeed, Malthus came close to making the very point himself, as suggested by his comment that unproductive consumers may 'furnish fresh motives to production, and tend to produce the wealth of a country further than it would go without them' (*M Works*, VI, p. 324).

The main, purely economic qualification to a government-financed programme concerns the alleged affects of 'high' levels of taxation. Thus, with regard to 'statesmen, soldiers, sailors, and those who live upon the interest of a national debt, it cannot be denied that they contribute powerfully to distribution and demand'; 'Yet', Malthus continued, 'to counterbalance these advantages ... it must be acknowledged that injudicious taxation might stop the increase of wealth at almost any period of its progress' (*M Works*, VI, p. 326). Moreover:

> taxation is a stimulus so liable in every way to abuse, and it is so absolutely necessary for the general interests of society to consider private property as sacred, that one should be extremely cautious of treating to any government the means of making a different distribution of wealth, with a view to the general good (*M Works*, VI, p. 327)

So, although it *might* be possible for the government to increase the general level of effectual demands by means of a taxation-financed transfer to unproductive labourers, the policy could run the risk of undermining the accumulation process either by reducing the capitalists' 'power' to accumulate (i.e. reducing profits) or by diminishing their 'will' if they perceived a threat to the existing structure of property relationships.

It is therefore *conceivable* that Malthus had grasped the rationale for a government-led expansion of effectual demand but rejected the policy on the grounds that the levels of taxation required would negate any possible benefits. A problem with this suggestion is, however, that Malthus at least hinted that *higher* taxes would be desirable in the post-war economic climate. Thus:

> The returned taxes, and the excess of individual gains above expenditure which were so largely used as revenue during the war, are now in part, and probably in

no inconsiderable part, saved. I cannot doubt, for instance, that in our own country very many persons have taken the opportunity of saving a part of their returned property tax .... This saving is quite natural and proper ... but still it contributes to explain the cause of the diminished demand for commodities, compared with their supply since the war. If some of the principal governments concerned spent the taxes which they raised in a manner to create a greater and more certain demand for labour and commodities, particularly the former, than the present owners of them ... we cannot be surprised at the duration of the effects arising from the transition from war to peace. (*M Works*, VI, p. 335)

An argument to the effect that higher taxation would increase the demand for labour and commodities (and not simply reduce supply) is certainly not incompatible with the position expressed in the above passage.

A further possibility is that, given certain other objectives, Malthus simply did not wish to advocate a policy of demand management, regardless of the taxation issue; or, as a variation on the same theme, perhaps he was so preoccupied with those other objectives that he was blind to the case for a government-led economic recovery. As I shall now argue, there is a case that can be made along these lines.

Malthus's 'bucolic' tendencies are well known. In the first edition of his *Essay* (1798), he famously declared himself as not 'a very determined friend' to trade and manufactures (*M Works*, I, p. 103) and, although his position softened over the years, he remained ever fearful of the growth in the manufacturing sector. An often repeated criticism of the manufacturing system was its detrimental effects on the health and virtue of those, particularly the labouring class, who worked within it.[42] But, perhaps more importantly, Malthus also argued that the labouring classes in manufacturing were especially prone to outbreaks of discontent and turmoil which were sparked by periodic fluctuations in employment.[43] Admittedly, there were compensations. The growth of trade and manufacturing had dissolved the bonds of direct dependence of labourers upon landlords, it had stimulated activity, and, above all, it had increased the proportion of the middle classes, 'that body on which the liberty, public spirit, and good government of every country must mainly depend' (*Observations on the Effects of the Corn Laws* (1814), (*M Works*, VII, p. 102).[44] And yet, those benefits notwithstanding, Malthus believed that the manufacturing sector (or, as he sometimes put it, the manufacturing *population*[45]) had assumed dangerous proportions. Hence, for example, his colourful pronouncement that the

body politic is in an artificial, and in some degree, diseased state, with one of its principal members out of proportion to the rest. (*Essay* ed 2 (1803); *M Works*, III, p. 679)

It was the 'diseased' growth of trade and manufacturing that he had in mind.

In view of Malthus's position on the 'undesirable' growth of non-agricultural activities, it would be odd to find him advocating a policy which would 'artificially' sustain their continued existence, let alone encourage their expansion. But there is a related, political consideration which presumably would have made such a policy even more unpalatable to him. I refer to his position on the popular reform movement.

There can be no doubt that Malthus was deeply troubled by the activities of the so-called 'radical reformers' (those, to cut the story short, who advocated annual parliaments, a secret ballot and 'universal' suffrage, if only for the adult male population). Thus, during the grim year of 1819,[46] he corresponded with Ricardo:

> I can hardly contemplate a more bloody revolution than I should expect would take place, if Universal suffrage and annual parliaments were effected by the intimidation of such meetings as have been latterly taking place.[47] These people have evidently been taught to believe that such a reform would completely relieve all their distresses; and when they found themselves, as they most certainly would, entirely disappointed, massacre would in my opinion go on till it was stopt by a military despotism. In the case of a revolution in this country, the distress would be beyond all comparison greater than in France. In France the manufacturing population was comparatively small, and the destruction of it which took place, was not so much felt; but in England the misery from want of work and food would be dreadful. I hope and trust however that these extremities may be avoided. (14 October 1819, *R Works*, VIII, pp. 107–8)

Here we meet again the problem that was raised in the 1817 edition of the *Essay* (see above, pp. 37–8) Against the contemporary background of the Tory government's renowned lassitude in the realms of 'distress-management' (coupled, one might add, with their equally well deserved reputation for draconian 'law and order' legislation[48]) it would have been political dynamite for Malthus to present a strong case in favour of remedial government intervention. It would also have been bizarre to find him, a supporter of the political status quo (by and large), willingly supplying the 'radicals' with such powerful ammunition. We should therefore not be surprised by his 'failure', or unwillingness, to have done so.

CONCLUSION

The principal conclusion of this chapter is that Malthus's reputation as a proto-Keynesian demand-manager stands in need of revision. Although it cannot be ruled out completely that Malthus envisaged *some* increase in the general level of effectual demand and hence in employment as a result of a public works programme, he certainly did not make a strong case – if any case at all – along those lines himself. Rather, the main economic benefit of the programme seems to have been its effect in diminishing the capital employed in productive activity and thus reducing the excess supply of material output. Whether Malthus *could* have made a case for a government-led recovery is another question, and one that may never be settled conclusively. I am inclined to think that he could indeed have done so and for two reasons choose not to: first, because he had no wish to shore up an 'overgrown' manufacturing sector (there were, for more reasons than one, too many producers); and second, because he was unwilling to play into the hands of the radical reformers. From my perspective, Malthus was the *frustrated* 'proto-Keynesian' whose theoretical work led him (if rather unsteadily) to conclusions from which he recoiled.

Ricardo presents a different case entirely. Whatever else may be said of his position, he at least had logic and unswerving conviction in support of the recommendation that the government should do precisely nothing against a background of collapsing markets and soaring unemployment. The problem was merely one of a momentary lapse of reason on the part of the capitalist class. With Malthus having spiked his own guns, Ricardo's victory was assured.

NOTES

1. Thus, in the opinion of Walter Eltis, Malthus was 'an early fine-tuner' who believed that 'extra government expenditure on, for instance, public works ... would [tend to] restore prosperity' (1984, pp. 140, 147) Samuel Hollander's version of Malthus's position is similar: 'Funds diverted from private capital outlays to be spent on public works ... would generate an increase in effectual demand for produce and accordingly stimulate an increase in the profit rate and ultimately in the demand for labour' (1969, p. 331). Cf. O'Leary (1942).
2. See Peach (1993), especially pp. 131–43.
3. The prefixes *R* and *M* are used to denote the *Collected Works* of Ricardo and Malthus respectively; roman letters are used in each case to denote the relevant volume.
4. This proposition had been advanced by Adam Smith who had claimed that the 'desire of food is limited in every man by the narrow capacity of the human stomach; but the desire of the conveniences and ornaments of building, dress, equipage, and household furniture, seems to have no limit or certain boundary' (1776, 1981, p. 181). Ricardo remarked in his *Principles* that he 'was, and am, deeply impressed with the truth of Adam's [Smith's] observation' (*R Works*, I, p. 387).
5. Ricardo's natural prices are defined by the condition of uniform wage and profit rates.
6. I emphasize 'tending' because Ricardo did allow for 'temporary' periods of excess demand for money and excess supply of commodities; for that reason, I have argued that the 'Say's equality' interpretation of Ricardo's version of the 'Law' is (weakly) preferable to the 'Say's identity' interpretation: see Peach (1993, pp. 140–1).
7. The natural wage is 'that ... which is necessary to enable the labourers, one with another, to subsist and to perpetuate their race, without either increase or diminution' (*R Works*, I, p. 93).
8. Indeed, the distress was so pervasive that, in a memorable parliamentary phrase, it was

   reported that labourers 'appear to be starving, as it were, in the midst of plenty' (Western, 7 March 1816; as reported in *Hansard*, vol. XXXIII, col. 41).

9. Brougham, 13 March 1817; as reported in *Hansard*, vol. XXV, col. 1007. The estimate should, perhaps, be taken with a pinch of salt, since it was presumably in the interest of the Whig opposition to play up the extent of the economic malaise.

10. See the reports of Ricardo's parliamentary speeches of 16 and 24 December 1819 (*R Works*, V, pp. 32–4, 38). As Samuel Hollander has observed, Ricardo's emphasis at this time on capital-deficiency rather than capital misallocation as an explanation for the distress was somewhat uncharacteristic (Hollander, 1979, p. 518).

11. The full title of Malthus's opus was, *Principles of Political Economy, Considered with a View to their Practical Application*. Reprinted as *M Works*, vols V and VI.

12. A useful introduction to 'effectual demand' (sometimes referred to by Malthus as 'effective demand') is provided by Adam Smith's conception of it as the quantity demanded by those who are both willing and able to purchase a commodity *at its natural price*. In turn, the natural price is the price which just repays the costs of production (wages, profit and rent) when they are at *their* natural rates: the ordinary or average rates at a given time and place. For Malthus, cost of production normally comprises of wages and profit alone. But, that difference aside, his concept of the effectual demand for a commodity is essentially the same as Smith's. Malthus's notion of *aggregate* effectual demand may be understood as the combined effectual demands for total material output.

13. See Malthus's letters to Ricardo of 6 July 1814, 19 August 1814, 11 September 1814, 9 October 1814 and 23 November 1814 (*R Works*, VI, pp. 111–12, 123, 132, 141–2, 155–6).

14. Consistently with his belief in an unlimited demand for luxuries and conveniences, Ricardo could not envisage any problem from employing 'all our soldiers, sailors and menial servants … in productive labour' (to Malthus, 18 December 1814, *R Works*, p. 164).

15. To recall, Ricardo's primary explanation of the distress ran in terms of the misallocation of resources. This finds some correspondence only with the third of the following grounds for Malthus's optimism.

16. That this was so is clear enough from the comments in the 1817 *Essay*; see also the correspondence quoted below, p. 46.

17. My synopsis is based on the *Principles*, *M Works*, VI, pp. 332–3.

18. As noted above, p. 32, Ricardo discounted any such effect.

19. Malthus claimed that the distress was even further aggravated by 'a sudden and extraordinary contraction of the currency' (*M Works*, VI, p. 332).

20. See *M Works*, VI, pp. 262, 319.

21. 'The varying rate of profit … depends upon the causes which alter the proportion between the value of the advances and the value of the produce; and this proportion may be altered either by circumstances which affect the value of the advances, or the value of the product' (*M Works*, V, p. 213).

22. Rashid (1977) has emphasized the point that Malthus's argument for the deficiency of effectual demand ran in terms of a general satiation of desires. However, while Malthus's account of the distress does imply that those in possession of the means to demand commodities had no wish to increase their consumption significantly, it also implies that many erstwhile demanders had ceased to consume *not* because they lacked the 'will', rather because they had lost the 'power': they had been ruined by the economic distress. The satiation problem was therefore the partial (but still fundamentally important) one that those currently in possession of the 'power' lacked the 'will' to increase significantly their consumption of goods and, less importantly, services.

23. See Ricardo's notes on Malthus's *Principles*, *R Works*, II, pp. 110–11, 313–14.

24. It might be added, however, that Ricardo's own account of the distress was also based on irrationality – a 'momentary lapse of reason' – since his capitalists *persist* in producing the 'wrong' commodities (i.e. those not suited to the unfulfilled desires of the potential demanders).

25. Cf: 'the symptoms appear to me exactly to resemble those which would arise from the sudden conversion of unproductive labour into productive, and the diminution of unproductive consumption; and … as a matter of opinion I am inclined to believe that if the

Stockholders in their new situation saved less and spent more profits would be higher and the stagnation of trade diminished' (Letter to Ricardo, 16 July 1821, *R Works*, IX, pp. 21–2).

26. Cf. Malthus's analysis of the effects of increasing the money supply as a possible way out of the depression: 'Perhaps a sudden increase of currency and a new facility of borrowing might under any circumstances, give a temporary stimulus to trade, but it would only be temporary. Without a large expenditure on the part of the government, and a frequent conversion of capital into revenue, the great powers of production acquired by the capitalists, operating upon the diminished power of purchasing possessed by the owners of fixed incomes, could not fail to occasion a still greater glut of commodities than is felt at present' (*M Works*, VI, p. 343).

27. The saving-investment relationship was affirmed quite explicitly by Malthus: 'it is stated by Adam Smith, and it must be allowed to be stated justly, that the produce which is annually saved is as regularly consumed, as that which is annually spent, but that it is consumed by a different set of people' (*Principles*, *Works*, V, p. 32). According to Blaug, with whom I concur, 'In the thousands of words that Malthus wrote on the question of general gluts, there are not more than a dozen that clearly express a theory of over-saving where saving is not identical to investment' (1985, p. 174).

28. See, for example, *M Works*, VI, pp. 253–4, 317.

29. See, for example, *R Works*, II, pp. 8–9, 302–3, 308–9, 310.

30. See, for example, *R Works*, II, pp. 302–3, 320–1, 429.

31. There appears to be a difference between this argument and the one advanced in the 1817 *Essay*. In the earlier work, the alleged problem was that the demand for manufactured objects of luxury and convenience would decline, although all the additional income of the tax beneficiaries would, it seems, be spent on *consumption* of one sort or another. See above, pp. 35–6.

32. See *M Works*, VI, pp. 264, 331, 333.

33. See, for example, *M Works*, V, pp. 35–6; VI, pp. 260–1, 293, 302–3.

34. Ricardo could never make sense of this argument, perhaps for good reason; he argued that the increase of exchangeable value must be accompanied by a reduction in *someone's* consumption. See *R Works*, II, p. 406.

35. 'In general it may be said that demand is quite as necessary to the increase of capital as the increase of capital is to demand. They mutually act upon and encourage each other, and neither of them can proceed with vigour if the other be left far behind.' (*M Works*, VI, p. 279).

36. 'One of the greatest benefits which foreign commerce confers ... is, its tendency to inspire new wants' (*M Works*, VI, p. 321).

37. 'Practically it has always been found that the excessive wealth of the few is in no respect equivalent, with regard to effective demand, to the more moderate wealth of the many. A large body of manufacturers and merchants can only find a market for their commodities among a numerous class of consumers above the rank of mere workmen and labourers. And experience shows us that manufacturing wealth is at once the consequence of a better distribution of property, and the cause of further improvements in such distribution, by the increase in the proportion of the middle classes of society ...'; and also: 'Thirty of forty proprietors, with incomes answering to between one thousand and five thousand a year, would create a more effective demand for [commodities] ... than a single proprietor possessing a hundred thousand a year ...' (*M Works*, VI, p. 299).

38. See *M Works*, VI, pp. 253–4, 322, 363.

39. As noted above, Ricardo's objection to this argument was that accumulation might continue providing that the rate of profit remains above its 'minimum' level.

40. The argument was stated thus: 'Almost all merchants and manufacturers save, in prosperous times, much more rapidly than it would be possible for the national capital to increase, so as to keep up the value of the produce. [Hence] ... they could not afford an adequate market to each other by exchanging their several products.

   'There must therefore be a considerable class of other consumers, or the mercantile classes could not continue extending their concerns, and realizing their profits. In this class the landlords no doubt stand pre-eminent; but if the powers of production among capitalists are considerable, the consumption of the landlords, in addition to that of the capitalists and ... [productive] workmen, may still be insufficient to keep up and increase the exchangeable value of the produce.' (*M Works*, VI, p. 319). Hence the need for unproductive consumers (in addition to the landlords). For Ricardo, however, 'A body of unproductive labourers are just as necessary and as useful with a view to future production, as a fire, which should consume in the manufacturers warehouse the goods which those unproductive labourers would otherwise consume' (*R Works*, II, p. 421).

41. Ricardo certainly interpreted Malthus's position along such lines. Thus: 'If his views on this question be correct – if commodities can be so multiplied that there is no disposition to purchase and consume them, then undoubtedly the cure which he hesitatingly recommends is a very proper one. If the people entitled to consume will not consume the commodities produced, themselves, nor cause them to be consumed by others ... we cannot do better than follow the advice of Mr Malthus, and oblige the Government to supply the deficiency of the people. We ought in that case to petition the King to dismiss his present economical ministers, and to replace them by others, who would more effectually promote the best interests of the country by promoting public extravagance and expenditure. We are it seems a nation of producers and have few consumers amongst us, and the evil has at last become of that magnitude that we shall be irretrievably miserable if the parliament or the ministers do not immediately adopt an efficient plan of expenditure' (*R Works*, II, p. 307).

42. See, for example: *Essay* (1798) (*M Works*, I, p. 112); *Observations on the Effects of the Corn Laws* (1815) (*M Works*, VII, p. 101); and the *Essay* (1817) (*M Works*, III, p. 445).

43. See, for example: *Essay* (1798) (*M Works*, I p. 112); *Observations on the Effects of the Corn Laws* (1814) (*M Works*, VII, p. 101); and *Essay* (1817) (*M Works*, III, p. 444). The fluctuations emphasized by Malthus were those arising from the caprices of taste, transitions from war to peace (and vice versa) and credit failures.

44. See also: *Essay* (1798) (*M Works*, I, p. 103); *Observations on the Effects of the Corn Laws* (1814) (*M Works*, VII, pp. 101–2); and *Essay* (1817) (*M Works*, III, pp. 401, 445).

45. *Essay* (1803) (*M Works*, III, p. 686); cf. Malthus's stated preference in the *Essay* (1803) for the maintenance of 'a balance between the agricultural and commercial *classes*' (*M Works*, III, pp. 423–4, emphasis added).

46. The leader of the opposition, Tierney, is reported to have described 1819 as witnessing 'a greater stagnation than was ever before known' (Smart, 1920, p. 689)

47. Malthus was apparently referring to the ill-fated meeting in Manchester, subsequently known as 'Peterloo'.

48. This was the year in which the government passed the notorious 'Six Acts'.

REFERENCES

Blaug, M. (1985), *Economic Theory in Retrospect*, Cambridge: Cambridge University Press.

Corry, B. (1959), 'Malthus and Keynes – A Reconsideration', *Economic Journal*, **69**, 717–24.

Eltis, W. (1984), *The Classical Theory of Economic Growth*, London: Macmillan.

Hollander, S. (1969), 'Malthus and the Post-Napoleonic Depression', *History of Political Economy*, **1**, 306–35.

Hollander, S. (1979), *The Economics of David Ricardo*, London: Heinemann.

Malthus, T.R. (1986), *The Works of Thomas Robert Malthus*, edited by E.A. Wrigley and D. Souden, London: William Pickering.

O'Leary, J. (1942), 'Malthus and Keynes', *Journal of Political Economy*, **50**, 901–19.

Peach, T. (1993), *Interpreting Ricardo*, Cambridge: Cambridge University Press.

Rashid, S. (1977), 'Malthus' Model of General Gluts', *History of Political Economy*, **9**, 366–83.

Ricardo, D. (1821, 1951–55), *The Works and Correspondence of David Ricardo*, edited by P. Sraffa with the collaboration of M.H. Dobb, Cambridge: Cambridge University Press,

Smart, W. (1910), *Economic Annals of the Nineteenth Century, 1801–1820*, London: Macmillan.

Smith, A. (1776, 1981), *An Inquiry into the Nature and Causes of the Wealth of Nations*, Indianapolis: Liberty Press.

3. From sunspots to social welfare: the unemployment problem 1870–1914

Jose Harris

DID IT EXIST?

One is tempted to deal briskly with theories of unemployment between 1870 and 1914 by saying that there were none. 'Unemployment' did not figure as an explicit problem in any of the great canonical or semi-canonical economic works of the period. It was largely ignored in the systematic writings of Jevons, Foxwell, Edgeworth and Alfred Marshall; and, perhaps more surprisingly, it played little part in the critique of the classical system launched by economists of the historical school, such as Cunningham, Ashley, and W.S. Hewins (Khadish, 1982). The word 'unemployment' was coined by Marshall almost accidentally in 1888, and seems to have rapidly seeped into popular usage (Marshall, 1926, p. 92; Hobson, 1895, pp. 315–32); but of the large number of reports, books and articles on the subject which began to pour forth from the mid-1890s none was written by an 'academic'[1] professional economist. They came instead from amateurs; from journalists, practical reformers, heretics and cranks – men like William Beveridge, Percy Alden, J.A. Hobson, and J.M. Robertson, none of whom had any serious standing as an economic theorist even though each was quite well-known in some other sphere. Throughout the period, the only English work specifically devoted to 'unemployment' to be written by a university-based economist was A.C. Pigou's little book in the Home University Library series that appeared in 1913 – largely for the benefit of a lay, popular readership. Pigou's study linked unemployment to a wide range of early 20th-century social concerns such as strikes, poverty, degeneracy and the treatment of the 'residuum'; but, for all this, it did little more than restate the classical proposition that unemployment was primarily a function of inelastic wage-rates (Pigou, 1913, pp. 79–93, 242–3). In this, and other works by British university-based economists, there was no serious theoretical challenge to, nor even tentative questioning of, the master paradigm of Ricardo and Adam Smith.

Despite its absence from canonical economic theory, however, 'want of employment' moved between 1870 and 1914 from being a minor problem on the fringes of the Poor Law to being one of the major social, political and administrative concerns of the age. During the 1860s, official cognizance of the existence of those who could not find work had been largely confined to the casual ward, to occasional emergency relief works (as in the Lancashire cotton famine) and to spasmodic efforts to encourage emigration. Neither orthodox economists nor official Poor Law theorists were ever quite so indiscriminately hostile to the able-bodied poor as their critics have supposed; but nevertheless there was a widespread assumption among those responsible for the Poor Law system that work was available somewhere if only the workless looked hard enough (an assumption that appeared to be borne out by the fact that, even at moments of acute trade depression, the 'able-bodied' looking for work were never more than a tiny minority of those applying for poor relief) (Royal Commission, 1911, pp. 22–3, 27, 44). Popular perceptions of and attitudes towards those out of work seem to have mirrored official scepticism. In the massive fact-finding operations of the mid-Victorian social-science movement the incidence of unemployment was largely ignored. And although there was much casual charity, the unemployed – unlike children, animals, prostitutes, the sick and the heathen – were not the objects of any of the great organized mid-Victorian philanthropic movements: on the contrary, private philanthropists no less than public officials dreaded the hazards of disincentives to mobility, interference with wages, premature procreation of children, and artificial creation of work.

Fifty years later, although Poor Law perspectives remained powerful, both official and popular perceptions of unemployment had changed on many fronts. The unemployed themselves, though still not free from personal moral censure, were increasingly regarded as victims of structural and cultural forces beyond their own control. And those structural and cultural forces were in turn viewed as being, if not wholly controllable, at least susceptible to political intervention and adaptation. Since the 1880s, local authorities throughout Great Britain had been under pressure from central government to concentrate their capital projects into periods of cyclical and seasonal depression – an approach powerfully endorsed by the terms of reference of the centralized Development and Road funds set up by the Treasury in 1910. Under the Labour Exchanges Act 1909 centrally-funded employment bureaux had been set up in all centres of industry. Two years later the Lloyd George National Insurance Act had introduced publicly-subsidized compulsory unemployment insurance for nearly three million workers – a scheme which Whitehall officials had every intention of eventually extending to the whole of the manual work-force. In addition, programmes for helping, organizing or disciplining the unskilled unemployed had for the first time begun to

attract the support of large-scale philanthropy. In the 1890s and 1900s volun-
tary-funded employment schemes, training schemes, back-to-the-land schemes
and various kinds of labour colony sprang up throughout Britain. Most of
these voluntary ventures were conspicuously unsuccessful in their practical
outcomes: but they suggest that popular and philanthropic attitudes to the
problem of unemployment had changed dramatically over the previous 40
years (Harris, 1972; Garraty, 1978, especially pp. 103–64; Topalov, 1994).
These shifts in policy and public sentiment were by no means confined to
Great Britain, but were paralleled in many other countries. An international
conference at the Sorbonne in September 1910 – organized by the ex-invest-
ment banker, Max Lazard – was attended by 582 delegates from 27 nations
(including 18 official government delegations and representatives of 193
voluntary institutions and charities). The conference led to the setting-up of a
permanent international association on unemployment, whose purpose was to
collect statistics and to share information about unemployment theories and
policies throughout the industrialized world (Topalov, 1994, pp. 59–115).

The material and political pressures behind these attitudinal and policy
changes cannot be dealt with in detail in this chapter. They were clearly
linked not merely to the intrinsic evolution of unemployment as an
acknowledged socio-economic problem, but to such wider factors as the
admission of working-class voters to the franchise, the crystallization of an
international trade cycle, and the emergence of much larger units of industrial organization. The agricultural depression and mass migration of the
1880s visibly accelerated and threw into sharp relief an invisible social
process that had been occurring for many generations, whereby the endemic
underemployment characteristic of rural society was replaced by the much
more sharply differentiated conditions of 'employment' and 'unemployment', characteristic of work in industrial occupations. Mass demonstra-
tions of the unemployed in the mid-1880s, the early 1890s and again in the
1900s did not frogmarch the governing classes into instant action, but they
did help to generate a climate of opinion in which unemployment was
defined as a 'problem': a problem not merely of economic analysis but,
even more pressingly, of political and moral order (Topalov, 1994, pp. 13–
35). Moreover, as a number of recent historians have emphasized, the
simultaneous emergence of 'unemployment' in all industrial countries in
the late 19th century was the product not merely of global cycles of economic activity but of more immediate human agency in the form of more
regular and routinized strategies of production and public administration.
Literacy, timekeeping, industrial discipline, standard wage-rates, safety-
regulations, age-stratification, the intellectual conventions of official statistics, and changing norms of motherhood and childhood all played their part
in clearly demarcating the boundaries of the labour market – and in sharp-

ening the definition of those who were 'in' and those who were 'out of' work (Whiteside, 1991, pp. 21–51; Topalov, 1994, pp. 15–58).

Such factors played a major role both in precipitating the growth of unemployment as a substantive problem, and in shaping its intellectual interpretation. As was suggested above, the direct input from 'grand theory' was negligible, except in so far as students of the problem felt constrained by the immense scientific and moral prestige of the political economy of a previous age. Yet it would be quite wrong to give the impression that the approach to unemployment at the end of the 19th century was merely one of pragmatic problem-solving – a 'Macdonagh model' in which facts 'spoke for themselves' and conditions became 'intolerable' without the intermediate role of thought and value-judgement. On the contrary, the attempt to measure and explain unemployment was closely bound up with some of the major intellectual movements of the period, and in the long-run – beyond the terminal date of this chapter – was to generate the most ambitious restatement of general economic theory since Adam Smith. In this chapter I shall try to avoid the pitfall of treating all theorizing about unemployment before 1914 as a kind of prelude to Keynesianism; but, nevertheless, themes that were eventually to be taken up and reworked by Keynes do constitute an important strand in the story. This chapter will review the development of ideas about unemployment before 1914 in the light of those wider intellectual movements. It will look first at the lesser writings of some of the mainstream economic theorists of the period, to see whether their thought was really quite so silent on the subject as is usually supposed. Second, it will consider the views of those who specifically rejected many tenets of the so-called classical system, and sought to reinterpret not merely unemployment but the totality of economic relationships in wholly different terms. And, third, it will examine the growth of a statistical and administrative tradition which tacitly accepted the underlying framework of classical political economy, but nevertheless reinterpreted many of the problems of the labour market, particularly unemployment, in a new, more active and 'interventionist' light.

THE ECONOMISTS

First, then, the observations of the economists themselves. As was emphasized above, no economist of the period incorporated unemployment into a general theory of economic behaviour. But this does not mean that they believed unemployment did not exist – nor that they necessarily ascribed it to irrational or immoral individual behaviour. On the contrary, even economists of the 1834 generation had often ascribed want of employment to the imperfect flow of market information and unwise government policies – or to archaic institutional and customary arrangements that were largely beyond the individual's personal control. As early as 1842, the Outdoor Relief Regulation Order – which allowed relief to those discharged during cyclical depressions without imposition of the 'workhouse test' – had tacitly admitted the inexorable fact of irregularity of employment in many industrial areas. In the 1860s and 1970s there was much criticism among economic writers of the over-confidence with which the earlier generation of economists had assumed an automatic equivalence between supply and demand (Hutchison, 1953, pp. 1–31); and throughout the period 1870 to 1914 many leading economists acknowledged the existence of unemployment as a major social, philanthropic and administrative problem even if they could not adequately account for it as an economic one. There was widespread acceptance of the fact that individual workers were often the victims of 'crashes and flushes', vagaries of fashion, bad industrial organization, and the obstinate refusal of governments, investors and consumers to observe sound economic doctrine. What is perhaps more interesting than this acknowledgement of economic pathology, however, is the occasional veiled hint from within the heartland of orthodox political economy that unemployment might be something more than this; that it might be in some sense intrinsic to the normal functioning of the economic system rather than an unaccountable deviation from the working of true economic laws.

These hints of heresy came from a number of unexpected quarters, of which the first and most unexpected was the much-derided 'sunspot' theory of W.S. Jevons. In many 'new liberal' reformist writings of the 1900s Jevons was to figure as the arch-enemy of new theories of social progress because his invention (or discovery) of 'marginalism' was deemed to have powerfully reinforced the rational-individualist model of economic behaviour at the expense of more structural, 'organic', or 'collectivist' themes. But, as some at least of the Edwardian reform movement were aware, Jevons had also tentatively outlined an approach to the unemployment question that moved far away from the realm of rational choice. In an address to the British Association meeting in Dublin in 1878, Jevons had linked fluctuations in economic activity to meteorological disturbances induced by volcanic eruptions on the surface of the sun (Jevons 1978, 1964, pp. 125–40). Ensuing changes in climatic conditions brought about agricultural failure in primary producing countries, which in turn triggered off periodical contractions in the spheres of industry and commerce. It was the action of these 'sunspots', Jevons suggested, rather than the mere psychology of human beings, that afforded the most fundamental explanation for the decennial 'manias and panics' that had characterized international economic activity for more than a hundred years.

The substance of Jevons's thesis gained little credence at the time and has afforded historians much scope for malice and mockery ever since. Yet, for the purposes of this chapter it matters less whether the sunspot theory was true or false than that it suggested certain novel approaches to problems of the labour market, and indeed to social problems more generally. At one level it may be seen as a very extreme statement of the kind of natural-science-based positivism which by the 1870s was rivalling the psychological positivism central to utilitarianism and classical political economy.[2] 'Surely', wrote Jevons in a phrase pregnant with ulterior philosophic meaning, 'we must go beyond the mind to its industrial environment': and, similarly, 'I can see no reason why the human mind, in its own spontaneous action, should select a period of just 10.44 years to work in' (Ibid., p. 133). Such an approach neither proved nor disproved the theory of sunspots: but it clearly signalled the shift away from personal to structural explanations of unemployment that was to characterize studies of the labour market in the 1890s and 1900s. Jevons's lecture also anticipated another important strand in Edwardian revisionist thought, by emphasizing a link between employment and levels of consumption: 'It is now well-known to manufacturers that an active demand for their produce is to be expected only when food is cheap ... the depressed trade of Lancashire at the present time is generally attributed to the slackness of the export trade to India, which is due to the scarcity of food in that country, this scarcity absorbing the whole earnings of the poorer classes' (Ibid., pp. 134–5).

Jevons's sunspot theory played no part in his *Theory of Political Economy*, which in many successive editions dismissed fears of a general 'over-production' as 'evidently absurd and self-contradictory' (Jevons, 1924, p. 202). But his Dublin lecture was reprinted many times over the next 40 years, and was well known to Edwardian students of the unemployment problem like Charles Booth, Hubert Llewellyn Smith and William Beveridge (particularly the latter, whose earliest writings on unemployment included an attempt to ground Jevons's theory of the trade cycle on a broader empirical and statistical base[3]) (Beveridge, 1907, pp. 160–70). Even Jevons's severest critic, J.A. Hobson, conceded that Jevons in giving priority to consumption had opened 'a gateway' into 'hitherto neglected country' (Hobson, 1914, p. 5). And, perhaps more importantly, Jevons's approach to the trade cycle and his interest in the motive power of consumption found certain echoes in the lesser writings of other mainstream economic theorists. In the midst of the depression of the 1880s a lecture by Jevons's disciple and posthumous editor, Professor H.S. Foxwell, advanced the view that lack of employment was largely outside the rational control of the individual unemployed. Foxwell ascribed the prevailing high level of unemployment to the world shortage of gold; the recovery of international trade was being hampered throughout the industrial world by inelastic supplies of currency and inadequate facilities for credit, which could only be cured by government intervention to expand the basis of money

(Foxwell, 1886). And in 1886 a number of university or city-based economists sitting on, or giving evidence to, the Royal Commission on the Depression of Trade and Industry blamed a wide variety of political and structural
factors – monetary, fiscal, cultural and meteorological – for the current shortfall of employment. Most of them echoed the classical view that 'a general
over-production is of course impossible'; but, in striking contrast to the views
prevalent in public enquiries 50 years earlier, scarcely any of them ascribed
lack of employment to inelastic wages, over-generous welfare payments, or
the sloth and immobility of the unemployed (Royal Commission, 1886).[4]

Employment problems also attracted the spasmodic attention of Professor
Alfred Marshall. In 1884, Marshall had written a much-quoted article on the
London poor, suggesting that there was a large body of inferior unemployed
workmen who were irredeemably surplus to the needs of an advanced industrial economy and who were therefore destined to be a permanent burden on
the rest of society. Such people were to be treated not as 'criminals', but as
the legitimate objects of incarceration in disciplinary labour camps and of
'uncompromising inspection and inquiry' (Marshall, 1884, pp. 224–31). Ten
years later, however, Marshall's evidence to the Royal Commission on the
Aged Poor presented the problem in a quite different light. Low wages and
lack of employment were now ascribed to a failure of effective demand – the
solution laying in more generous social welfare payments and other forms of
redistribution of income. If 'a mad Emperor of China' were gratuitously to
distribute half-crowns to all the people of England, then the result would be,
not the depression of wages and collapse of incentives envisaged by orthodox
Poor Law theory, but increased demand, higher wages, improved living standards, and a general upward spiral of aspiration, education and civilization,
which would restore the unemployed to full participation in civic and economic life (Marshall, 1926, pp. 227, 248–50).[5]

Marshall's statement to the Aged Poor Commission may perhaps be read
as symptomatic of a much wider shift of opinion among the charitable public
on questions of redistribution of income. However, Marshall gave evidence to
the Commission, not in his role as a professor of economics but as a repre-
sentative of the Cambridge branch of the Charity Organisation Society. It was
significant that, just as in the case of Jevons, Marshall's efforts to explain
want of employment in terms, first of degeneracy and later of deficient
consumption, were not reflected in his major theoretical works. The mad
Emperor of China had not even a walking-on part in Marshall's *The Economics of Industry* or *Principles of Economics*, and Marshall's private correspondence suggests that in general he was inclined to view unemployment
less as an economic question than as a subject for ethics, biology or sociology (Pigou, 1925, pp. 426–7). A similar point may be made about the successor to Marshall's Cambridge chair, Professor A.C. Pigou. As noted above,

Pigou wrote a popular handbook on the unemployment question, and he lectured to the 1910 Paris conference on 'Le probleme de l'inactivité involontaire' (Topalov, 1994, p. 92). In 1909 he embarked upon the immensely ambitious task of trying to construct a theoretical foundation for the policy of the 'National Minimum' advanced by the Fabian socialists, Sidney and Beatrice Webb (Royal Commission, 1910a, pp. 981–1000). The fruit of this work was Pigou's *Wealth and Welfare* (1912) – a book that ranks as a major landmark in the development of 'welfare economics'; yet this study scarcely mentioned the existence of unemployment (even though abolition of unemployment was a cornerstone of the 'National Minimum' programme envisaged by the Webbs). All this seems to confirm the fact that, although professional economists of this period were by no means oblivious to unemployment, they were either unwilling or unable to incorporate it into their systems of grand theory. Their writings on unemployment were either fragmentary *jeux d'esprit*, or they were part of a much wider public debate to which economists happened to contribute as private citizens or social reformers rather than as specialists in economic theory. We must therefore look elsewhere for a fuller picture of the emergence of unemployment from the recesses of the Victorian Poor Law to the forefront of Edwardian social and political debate.

THE HERETICS

Second, then, the heretics – those who rejected the notion of a full-employment equilibrium, either as categorically wrong or as culturally specific to an earlier epoch of economic activity. It is enshrined in progressive folklore that nobody who held such views could obtain a post in any British university during the period under review; but this story seems scarcely credible, since such prominent institutions as the universities of Oxford, Glasgow and Birmingham and the infant London School of Economics all housed certain professors who belonged to the 'historical' or even 'socialist' schools of economic thought. Nevertheless, it is true that the major critique of the classical position on unemployment came from theorists and writers who were not professionally employed as economists and were not attached to any university department. The main reason for the exclusion of this group appears to have been not the fact that their doctrines were intrinsically unorthodox (the same would have been true of William Smart at Glasgow or Thorold Rogers at Oxford) but that they practised a discipline which many found hard to recognize as 'economics'. Their prophet was not Adam Smith but John Ruskin; and like Ruskin they believed that economics should be not an analytical discipline derived from certain sharply-defined premises about one area of human behaviour, but a broad, cultural and ethical discipline whose boundaries were coterminous with the whole of human life. For social reformers in late-Victorian and Edwardian Britain, this approach to economic doctrine proved a far more magnetic alternative to classical theory than the ideas put forward by Karl Marx – whose economic writings, available in English since the 1880s, were largely dismissed by reviewers not as a revolutionary challenge to capitalist economics but as a rather old-fashioned and eccentric variant of the familiar classical tradition.

John Ruskin, however, was another matter. Ruskin's works reached their peak of circulation and popularity, not in the 1850s and 1860s when he had been a major figure in the intellectual and cultural life of London's learned societies and salons, but during the decade after his death in 1900. Ruskin's writings on economic themes – 'Munera Pulveris', 'Unto this Last', 'The Political Economy of Art' – were reprinted in the 1890s and 1900s in many popular editions, and were widely studied in the university extension movement, the labour movement, the ethical movement, and in the numerous civic reform movements that were a central feature of community life in much of Edwardian Britain. Even the Charity Organisation Society, reputedly a bastion of orthodox *laissez-faire* ideas, nevertheless used Ruskin's works as their primary source for the teaching of 'social economics'.[6] Ruskin's economic thought cannot be discussed in detail here, but there were many features of it that were of relevance to the history of ideas about unemployment: most notably his rejection of a utilitarian psychology of work, his insistence that it was consumption rather than anticipation of profit which created jobs, his claim that 'saving' was useless unless it found an outlet in production, his recommendation of compulsory discipline and training for those who refused the ethical duty of work, and his belief that 'guilds' and 'communities' should ultimately replace 'firms' and 'markets'. Above all, Ruskin had rejected root and branch the principle of division of labour: it was precisely the 'sauntering' between tasks which Smith had condemned in pre-industrial employments that Ruskin believed gave 'joy' and 'meaning' to the natural human occupation of 'work' (Ruskin, 1912, pp. 38–80, 171–202, 295–321).[7]

All these ideas were to resonate through the turn-of-the-century unemployment debate, though with varying degrees of practical influence. The numerous attempts to employ the unemployed in various forms of non-market production that sprang up all over Britain in the 1890s and 1900s drew their ideas directly from Ruskin: indeed, the leader of the labour colony movement, Dr John Paton, was one of Ruskin's most ardent apostles (Marchant 1909). Sidney Webb's vision of replacing employment through the market by 'salaried public service, with the stimulus of duty and esteem' was explicitly inspired by Ruskin (Webb, 1891, p. 249). Ruskin's attack on excessive saving was echoed in a book published in 1892 by J.M. Robertson, editor of the radical weekly *The National Reformer* and later to be Parliamentary Secretary at the Board of Trade (Robertson, 1892). But Ruskin's major disciple in the sphere of unemployment was to be his biographer and popularizer, J.A. Hobson, perhaps the most influential economic 'heretic' of the Edwardian generation. Although Hobson was not uncritical of Ruskin's vagueness and grandeur, he was convinced, like Ruskin, that it was impossible to separate 'economics' from art and ethics; and he was to spend a lifetime expanding and elaborating Ruskin's claim that 'there is no wealth but life' (Hobson, 1914, 1920, 1929). For our purposes, the most important theme that Hobson extracted from Ruskin was the theory of under-consumption, which he developed in a series of books and articles published between 1889 and 1896 (the same years in which he was also preparing his quasi-biographical study of Ruskin's social thought (Hobson 1899). In these works Hobson set out to refute the view that in a properly functioning competitive economy the normal state of the labour market was one of full employment. Instead he argued that not just labour but land and capital were suffering from simultaneous underemployment, caused by a chronic deficiency of consumer demand. This 'under-consumption' was in turn caused by excessive saving, which Hobson ascribed to a top-heavy distribution of national income: thus the poor could not convert their needs into purchase of goods and services, while the rich could not find outlets for their savings and were compelled to invest abroad. The solution lay in the development of home markets by redistribution to lower income groups and employment-creating public works (Hobson and Mummery, 1895a, pp. 415–32; 1895b, pp. 744–60; 1896).

Hobson's theory of under-consumption constituted the most ambitious and far-reaching general analysis of the unemployment problem published during the period under review. In popular debate it rapidly permeated not just the unemployment question but many other aspects of Edwardian social concern – old-age pensions, tax reform, and the much wider question of 'economic imperialism' (Freeden, 1978, pp. 117–244). Among literate working men it helped to fuel endemic scepticism about the moral and intellectual claims of traditional political economy. Yet it made little immediate dent upon the economic literature and – contrary to what has sometimes been claimed – there is little evidence to suggest that it had any major impact at the time on official perceptions of unemployment. Orthodox Whitehall economists like Robert Giffen made short work of the claim that unemployment was causally linked to overseas investment – retorting that the latter actively created employment by opening up foreign markets to British goods (Giffen, 1905, pp. 483–93). I have never come across the slightest breath of Hobsonianism in any Treasury document of the period; and although Winston Churchill – who, as President of the Board of Trade, was minister in charge of unemployment policy – certainly favoured counter-cyclical public works, he did not link them with redistribution or under-consumption (PRO LAB 2/211 LE 500 1909b). More surprisingly, Hobson's fellow under-consumptionist, J.M. Robertson, left no visible mark on unemployment policy during his four years as a junior minister at the Board of Trade. And among reformist civil servants many who shared Hobson's sympathies nevertheless found his analysis fundamentally implausible: Beveridge, for example, thought that there was 'nothing in Hobson' that could not be better explained as a problem of inefficient management (Beveridge, 1910, p. 59). To understand changes in the official mind we must therefore turn to the third wing of unemployment thought that developed during this period: the views of those who saw it primarily as a problem of social welfare, industrial organization and rational public administration.

THE RATIONAL-BUREAUCRATS

The 'administrative' response to unemployment was developed over a long period of time by those whose primary concern was not with abstract theory, but with unemployment as an adjunct to the day-to-day management of pauperism and poverty. This is not to suggest that their perspective was purely pragmatic, but that their concern with theories and principles was not exclusively economic in character. As mentioned above, official Poor Law policy towards the unemployed was always potentially flexible in times of crisis; but signs of a more principled and permanent revision of Poor Law theory had begun to emerge in the 1860s – initially as a response to public indignation about the Poor Law's refusal to discriminate between the 'deserving' and the 'undeserving'.[8] Pamphlets and official reports of the 1860s and 1870s increasingly distinguished between a delinquent underclass of 'professional' unemployed who made a living from begging and exploitation of charity, and a class of 'virtuous' unemployed who were the victims of unpredictable industrial misfortune (Greenwood, 1868, 1976; Hill, 1875, pp. 656–73). The pursuit of different strategies towards these two classes was the main rationale of the Charity Organisation movement, which gained official recognition from the Local Government Board in 1869 and was to exert considerable influence over central and local government policies until the end of the century. From the mid-1880s, however, the moral perspective of the Charity Organisation Society was increasingly challenged and rivalled by other administrative themes. The plight of the virtuous unemployed increasingly acquired not merely moral but civic significance, as a corollary of successive extensions of the franchise. The famous Chamberlain circular issued by the Local Government Board in 1886 acknowledged the fact that, even among the unskilled and casual poor, there was much genuine 'distress from want of employment' for which poor relief was no longer a politically acceptable panacea. Towards the end of the 1880s, Charles Booth began his monumental empirical study of the 'labour and life' of the people of London – which was to conclude that, except for a tiny degenerate minority, unemployment in the lower reaches of the labour market was largely the product of bad industrial organization (Booth, 1902, 1969, vol. I, pp. 131–71; vol. XVII, pp. 204–10). Between 1886 and 1893 the Labour Bureau (later Labour Department) of the Board of Trade began for the first time to collect non-Poor Law based official statistics about levels of employment: figures which revealed that in times of commercial crisis more than 10 per cent of the normally employed work force might be thrown out of work. These figures were based on the returns of skilled trade unions who ran 'out-of-work' benefit schemes – schemes which in their turn played a major role in the shaping of public attitudes and in defining and legitimizing the unemployment problem. In essence, trade union benefit schemes were closely linked to protection of standard wage-rates in periods of recession; but during the 1880s many people who were normally suspicious of the trade union movement began to concede that there was some virtue in a system which kept a skilled work force together – at no expense to the public or to employers – for re-employment when economic activity began to revive. Moreover, the very high levels of occasional unemployment experienced by engineers, boilermen, carpenters and joiners underlined the fact that in a complex industrial economy inability to find work was in no way confined to misfits and moral failures. On the contrary, workmen who shared in out-of-work donation schemes were increasingly regarded as national economic and moral assets – economically they were valuable 'human capital', morally they were the finest flowering of the late-Victorian ethic of labour-aristocrat self-help (Royal Commission, 1910a, appendix xxi).

These various strands of new thought about the unemployed came together in a series of House of Commons committees that investigated 'distress from want of employment' in the parliamentary sessions of 1995 and 1996. These committees were a crisis response to the very severe winters of the early 1890s which generated widespread short-term unemployment throughout the country and compounded the existing longer-term recession. The committees made no immediate impact on public policy, but they played a major role in projecting the problem into the forefront of public debate – not least by popularizing the use of the term 'unemployment', which in 1894 was still an awkward neologism, but two years later had been absorbed into the conventional social vocabulary of the age. The evidence supplied to these committees by expert witnesses also helped to define the intellectual construction of the subject over the next 20 years. Foremost among these witnesses were Charles Booth himself, and one of Booth's former research assistants, now head of the Board of Trade's Labour Department, Hubert Llewellyn Smith. Both these men conceded the strength of a classical analysis of the unemployment problem; but both were also committed to the view that in the real historical and institutional world there were thousands of practical impediments to an effective market for labour. Habit, custom, vested interests, lack of information, imperfect education and training, and the perverse economic policies of Britain's trade rivals: all these were facts about the industrial world largely discounted by traditional economic theory but which students of modern industry had to take into account. Both Booth and Llewellyn Smith therefore viewed the problem primarily as one of classification and rational organization. Unemployment needed to be broken down into its component parts – cyclical, seasonal, structural and casual – and the unemployed themselves needed to be classified according to skill, type of unemployment, and past habits of regularity and economic independence. Depressions and cyclical fluctuations had to be recognized, not as economic disasters but as healthy natural occurrences inseparable from progress and industrial innovation. Unemployment had to be conceptually separated from the problem of poverty, since those thrown out of work were not necessarily 'poor', but they did face problems of rational budgeting over time. Above all, the labour market itself needed to be streamlined, 'decasualized' and physically reorganized. Instead of 'tramping in search of work' and the random recruitment of labour at the factory gate, there needed to be regular contracts of employment, formal channels of information about available jobs, and schemes for the redeployment of those made permanently redundant by the never-ending process of industrial change. Only thus could market forces fulfil their proper function and produce the 'full-employment equilibrium' envisaged by the classic theorists of 80 years before (Select Committee 1895; Booth, 1892, pp. 524–8; Llewellyn Smith, 1893).

This organizational approach to the labour market dominated official understanding of unemployment down to World War I: an approach reinforced by the fact that, when it came to the making of government policy, the only interest groups seriously consulted by ministers were representatives of skilled trade unions and employers' federations. When Beveridge in the late-1900s put forward his schemes for a national system of labour exchanges and compulsory decasualization of dock labour he claimed that he was merely seeking to extend, by use of state power, the rational processes of communication and organization which had been developed spontaneously within the most advanced sectors of the economy over the previous 50 years (Royal Commission, 1910a, QQ. 77831–79; 1910b, appendix xxi). Similarly, the Webbs' scheme for 'reorganisation of the labour market', promoted through the Royal Commission on the Poor Laws in 1909, treated the problem not as one of defective demand, but as one in which supply and demand for labour could be forced by administrative fiat into harmony with each other (Webb, 1909). The International Conference on Unemployment in 1910 – bent on maintaining its credibility by emphasizing the 'scientific' rather than 'political' character of the problem – gave priority to policies which focused on industrial and administrative organization (Topalov, 1994, pp. 73–5). And in 1911 the philosophy of national insurance, which treated cyclical unemployment as a normal, inevitable and in many ways desirable feature of a progressive economic system, drew heavily upon the analysis of the labour market advanced by Booth and Llewellyn Smith 16 years before. Moreover, one of the major aims of national insurance was not mere relief of need, but 'organization' as a good in its own right – as a process which it was believed would automatically help to reduce unemployment by promoting information, classification and registration of the work force, and by fostering closer relations between employers and employed (Beveridge, 1908).

AN OVERVIEW

Recognition of unemployment as a 'problem' therefore emerged from a variety of intellectual traditions that were by no means exclusively 'economic' in character. Indeed, economic theory played a very muted role in defining the problem; and concern about the social and political impact of unemployment continually ran ahead of the abstract conceptualization and theorization of the term. Though 'experts' on the subject were anxious to give their enquiries the status of a 'science', they rarely looked to economic theory to perform that function: instead they looked to statistics, sociology and public administration. Among administrators and politicians, and among the vast majority of economists, the treatment of unemployment was viewed first and foremost as an issue in 'social' and 'industrial' policy rather than as a problem in macroeconomics. This did not mean that conceptions of the problem were more subjective or sentimental than in previous generations: on the contrary, from Jevons's sunspot theories of the 1870s through to the social insurance schemes of the 1900s the inclination of many who grappled with the unemployment question was to use 'hard' techniques borrowed from the natural sciences rather than the more subjective criteria of the social worker or philanthropist. Board of Trade archives suggest that ministers and officials had every hope that, once the insurance system was firmly in place for regular workers, they would then be able to pursue far more draconian policies towards the unemployable 'residuum' (PRO LAB. 2/211 LE 500 1909c) (policies which had been advocated at various times by representatives of all the three intellectual traditions identified above). The need for such policies was often cited as proof of the fact that the issue was not primarily an economic one; and, except among self-confessed economic heretics, there was little sense that classical economic theory had failed to define or to answer the unemployment question. Among administrators, the dominant approach to unemployment was neither classical nor proto-Keynesian but overwhelmingly 'Weberian', in that it was seen largely as a problem of systemic rationality – the solution of which would leave the market system very largely intact. The Labour Exchanges Act of 1909, claimed Winston Churchill, was not a measure for the 'relief of distress': it was 'a mathematical and scientific proposition to give to labour that same market for the sale of labour that every other commodity has secured for itself' (PRO LAB, 2/211 LE 500 1909a). And, within this process, the 'permanent impartial Government official – with the growth of his business as his one principle aim' was the key to the effective management of all aspects of the problem (PRO LAB. 2/211 LE 499). More subversive ideas *were* put forward, which hinted at a more radical bouleversement of economic theory; but in this period their impact was largely ethical and cultural rather than political or economic. The analysis of approaches to unemployment between 1870 and 1914 therefore offers many insights into the untidy processes of second-order intellectual, social and administrative change: it has surprisingly little to say about specifically 'economic' policy, or about the making and breaking of grand paradigms in economic theory.

NOTES

1. Though one must acknowledge the rather ill-defined nature of academic economics in this period, when many who were loosely spoken of as 'economists' held university posts in other disciplines, such as classics, history and mathematics.
2. Jevons's paper had very strong resonances of the claims being put forward by Dr John Tyndall, also to the British Association, for the intellectual hegemony of a wholly deterministic 'natural science'. This is not to deny that Jevons was also a major figure in reinforcing 'positivisim' of the psychological variety.
3. A similar concern may be detected in Beveridge's lifelong interest in the history of food prices, in which he was still searching for the secret of the trade cycle as late as the 1960s.
4. Economists and writers on economic questions participating on the Commission included Bonamy Price, R.H. Inglis Palgrave, H.H. Gibbs, and Alfred Marshall.
5. Marshall's argument related specifically to the employment of the elderly and their position in the work force. His evidence also showed that he was still concerned with the problem of a degenerate and superfluous residuum; but he had become convinced that stern policies towards this group would be politically impossible until public opinion had been convinced that 'just' policies were being pursued towards those in genuine need.
6. Ruskinian 'social economics' rather than orthodox political economy was taught at the Charity Organisation Society's School of Sociology, founded in 1903 and absorbed into the London School of Economics in 1912.
7. For Ruskin's argument that the 'right to work' necessarily entailed the 'direction and discipline' of labour, see particularly *The Political Economy of Art*, pp. 11, 15.
8. Contrary to what is often believed, and faithfully reproduced by generations of writers on

the subject, the 1834 Poor Law did *not* differentiate between the 'deserving' and 'undeserving' poor: it merely offered relief on unattractive terms to anyone who felt themselves to be destitute. This system broke down because public opinion increasingly rejected the mechanistic equality meted out to victims of misfortune and semi-criminals. It was not so much desire to punish the 'undeserving' that led to new social policies, and ultimately to the early days of the 'welfare state', but desire to protect and privilege the 'deserving'.

REFERENCES

Beveridge, W. (1907), 'The Pulse of the Nation', *Albany Review*, **2**, 160–70.
Beveridge, W. (1908), leading articles in *Morning Post*, 8 and 29 May.
Beveridge, W. (1910), *Unemployment. A Problem of Industry*, London: Longmans.
Booth, C. (1892), 'Inaugural Address', *JRSS*, **55**, 524–8.
Booth, C. (1902, 1969), *Life and Labour of the People of London*, vols I and XVII, London: Macmillan. Reprinted New York: Augustus Kelley.
Foxwell, H.S. (1886), 'Irregularity of Employment and Fluctuations of Prices', in John Burnett *et al.*, *The Claims of Labour*, Edinburgh: Edinburgh Co-operative Print Co.
Freeden, M. (1978), *The New Liberalism. An Ideology of Social Reform*, Oxford: Clarendon Press.
Garraty, J.A. (1978), *Unemployment In History. Economic Thought and Public Policy*, New York: Harper and Row.
Giffen, R. (1905), 'Notes on Imports *versus* Home Production, and Home *versus* Foreign Investments', *Economic Journal*, **15**, 483–93.
Greenwood, J. (1868, 1976), *A Night in the Workhouse*. Reprinted in Peter Keating (ed.), *Into Unknown England 1886–1913*, London: Fontana.
Harris, J. (1972), *Unemployment and Politics. A Study in English Social Policy 1886–1914*, Oxford: Clarendon Press.
Hill, A.H. (1875), 'Unemployed Labour. What Means are Practicable for Checking the Aggregation and Deterioration of Unemployed Labour in Large Towns?', *Transactions of the National Association for the Promotion of Social Science*, 656–73.
Hobson, J.A. (1895), 'The Meaning and Measure of Unemployment', *Contemporary Review*, **67**, March, 315–32.
Hobson, J.A. (1899), *John Ruskin Social Reformer*, London: James Nisbet.
Hobson, J.A. (1914), *Work and Wealth. A Human Valuation*, London: Routledge.
Hobson, J.A. (1920), 'Ruskin as Political Economist', in J.H. Whitehouse (ed.), *Ruskin the Prophet*, London: E.P. Dutton and Co.
Hobson, J.A. (1929), *Wealth and Life*, London: G. Allen and Unwin.
Hobson, J.A. and Mummery, A.F. (1889), *The Physiology of Industry*, London: J. Murray.
Hobson, J.A. and Mummery, A.F. (1895a), 'The Meaning and Measure of Unemployment', *Contemporary Review*, **67**, March, 415–32.
Hobson, J.A. and Mummery, A.F. (1895b), 'The Economic Causes of Unemployment', *Contemporary Review*, May, 744–60.
Hobson, J.A. and Mummery, A.F. (1896), *The Problem of the Unemployed. An Enquiry and an Economic Policy*, London: Routledge.
Hutchison, T.W. (1953), *A Review of Economic Doctrines 1870–1926*, Oxford: Clarendon Press.
Jevons, W.S. (1878, 1964), 'The Periodicity of Commercial Crises and its Physical

Explanation'. Reprinted in R.L. Smyth (ed.), *Essays in the Economics of Socialism and Capitalism*, London: Gerald Duckworth.

Jevons, W.S. (1924), *The Theory of Political Economy*, London: Macmillan.

Khadish, A. (1982), *The Oxford Economists in the Late Nineteenth Century*, Oxford: Clarendon Press.

Llewellyn Smith (1893), *Agencies and Methods for Dealing with the Unemployed*, Cmnd 7182/1893–4.

Marchant, J. (1909), *J.B. Paton MA DD. Educational and Social Pioneer*, London: James Clarke and Co.

Marshall, A. (1884), 'The Housing of the London Poor', *Contemporary Review*, **45**, 224–31.

Marshall, A. (1926), *Official Papers*, edited by J.M. Keynes, London: Macmillan.

Pigou, A.C. (1912), *Wealth and Welfare*, London: Macmillan.

Pigou, A.C. (1913), *Unemployment*, London: Williams and Norgate, Home University of Modern Knowledge.

Pigou, A.C. (ed.) (1925), *Memorials of Alfred Marshall*, London: Macmillan.

PRO LAB.2/211 LE 499 (1909), 'Deputation of the Federation of Shipbuilding and Engineering Trades' Unions', 16 December, Beveridge's brief for Winston Churchill.

PRO LAB.2/211 LE 500 (1909a–c), 17 June, 'Board of Trade Conference with the Parliamentary Committee of the TUC'; 18 June, 'Report of the Conference with the Federation of Engineering and Shipbuilding Trades' Unions'; 18 August, 'Board of Trade Conference with the Engineering Employers' Association and the Shipbuilding Employers' Federation'.

Robertson, J.M. (1892), *The Fallacy of Saving*, London: Swan Sonnenschein and Co.

Royal Commission on the Depression of Trade and Industry (1886), *Final Report and Dissenting Memoranda*, Cmnd 4893.

Royal Commission on the Poor Laws (1910), Cmnd 5068 XLIX, appendix xxi (C) and lxxx, 981–1000 (1910b), minutes of evidence QQ. 77831–79 Cmnd 5066.

Royal Commission on the Poor Laws (1911), Cmnd 5077.

Ruskin, J. (1912), 'The Political Economy of Art', 38–80 'Unto This Last', 171–202 'The Crown of Wild Olive', 295–321 in Macmillan edn, *Ruskin's Political Economy of Art Etc.*, London: Macmillan.

Select Committees on Distress from Want of Employment (1895–6), H. of Cmnd 111, 253, 365.

Topalov, C. (1994), *Naissance du Chômeur 1880–1910*, Paris: Albin Michel.

Webb, S. (1891, 1902), 'The Difficulties of Individualism', *Economic Journal*, June. Reprinted in S. and B. Webb, *Problems of Modern Industry*, London: Longmans, Green and Co.

Webb, S. and Webb, B. (eds) (1909), *The Public Organisation of the Labour Market. Being Part Two of the Minority Report of the Poor Law Commission*, London: Longmans, Green and Co.

Whiteside, N. (1991), *Bad Times. Unemployment in British Social and Political History*, London: Faber.

4. The Treasury view in the interwar period: an example of *political* economy?*

George Peden

INTRODUCTION

The Treasury view of the interwar period is unusual among economic doctrines in that it derives its name from a government department rather than from a professional economist, or group of economists. The best known expression of the Treasury view is to be found in Winston Churchill's budget speech in 1929 (*Hansard*, 1929):

> The orthodox Treasury view ... is that when the Government borrow(s) in the money market it becomes a new competitor with industry and engrosses to itself resources which would otherwise have been employed by private enterprise, and in the process raises the rent of money to all who have need of it.

There were, the chancellor explained, circumstances in which government borrowing could be justified, but then the onus was on the government to prove that the expenditure was necessary or 'that the spending of the money by the Government would produce more beneficial results than if it had been left available for trade and industry'. Churchill pointed to recent government expenditure on public works such as housing, roads, telephones, electricity supply, and agricultural development, as well as guarantees for exports and colonial development, and concluded that, although expenditure for these purposes had been justified:

> for the purpose of curing unemployment the results have certainly been disappointing. They are, in fact, so meagre as to lend considerable colour to the

*This chapter is part of a wider research project intended to lead to a book on the British Treasury and public policy in the period 1906–59. My thanks are due to the British Academy and to All Souls College, Oxford, for appointing me to a research readership and a visiting fellowship respectively, and to the Leverhulme Trust and the Wolfson Foundation for meeting the cost of the research.

orthodox Treasury doctrine which has been steadfastly held that, whatever might be the political or social advantages, very little additional employment and no permanent additional employment can in fact and as a general rule be created by State borrowing and State expenditure.

These carefully drafted words reflected the official Treasury's view on proposals, associated with the Liberal leader, Lloyd George, and with John Maynard Keynes, for an employment policy based upon large-scale borrowing to finance public works. It is generally acknowledged that the theoretical basis of the Treasury view was set out by Ralph Hawtrey, the Treasury's only economist in the interwar period, in an article in *Economica* in 1925 (Clarke, 1988, pp. 51–3, 63; Howson and Winch, 1977, p. 27; Moggridge, 1992, p. 463). Hawtrey argued that normally government expenditure financed by borrowing from the public would merely crowd out an equivalent amount of private investment, by raising interest rates, unless additional bank credit were created. Hawtrey believed that, provided that business showed a normal degree of enterprise, the creation of bank credit alone would be sufficient to increase employment, and that public works would be unnecessary (Hawtrey, 1925). It should be noted that in the 1920s a deliberate expansion of bank credit was commonly described as inflation, which was then defined as an expansion of the supply of money to spend relative to the supply of things to purchase. It was only in the 1930s that the term 'reflation' came into use.

The Treasury view that borrowing to finance public works would tend to crowd out private investment was central to economic policy debates as the world moved into depression, and Keynes's efforts to demolish it played a significant part in the development of his *General Theory of Employment, Interest and Money* in the 1930s (Clarke, 1988; Moggridge, 1992; Skidelsky, 1992). Even in the 1920s there was very little support among professional economists for the Treasury view, most pre-Keynesians, notably A.C. Pigou, being primarily concerned with the high level of real wages, low productivity, and the apparent inability or unwillingness of many workers to respond to structural changes in demand (Casson, 1983).

During the period of Keynesian ascendancy in the British economics establishment after World War II, the Treasury view seemed to have been thoroughly discredited. Donald Winch, for example, while conceding that the weakness of Britain's balance of payments position, and her return to a fixed and overvalued exchange rate in 1925, provided some justification for the Treasury view, concluded that the real difficulty had been that officials had been unable to cope with Keynes's theoretical arguments on an intellectual level (Winch, 1969; pp. 109–13). In the 1970s, however, the experience of 'stagflation' made it respectable for economists to argue that public expenditure could crowd out private investment, even at a time of rising unemployment. Moreover, the availability to researchers, under the 30 years rule, of

Treasury and Cabinet papers made it possible to study the Treasury's arguments in greater detail than had been possible on the basis of published statements, although the full story of the formulation of the Treasury view could only be pieced together once a key file (PRO, 1929a) was belatedly transferred to the Public Record Office in 1986 (Clarke, 1988; pp. 47–69). Writing in a new economic environment, and with new evidence at their disposal, even economic historians who were not unsympathetic to Keynes were prepared to argue that there was some merit in the Treasury's case, in so far as it pertained to practical politics and administration, and financial confidence (Middleton, 1982, 1985; Peden, 1984).

I do not intend to repeat these arguments here. Instead, I wish to address two questions: first, what connection was there between the Treasury view and the doctrines of professional economists? And, second, to what extent was the Treasury view modified in the interwar period in response to the experience of unemployment and criticism by professional economists? The answers to both questions suggest that the Treasury view of 1929 was as much a product of traditions of public finance and of the City as of Hawtrey's economic theory. It is, I admit, difficult to be dogmatic about the relative importance of public finance and theory, since the rules of public finance were based, at least in part, on what Keynes called 'defunct economists' (1973a, p. 383). Moreover, Hawtrey himself developed his theory within the context of traditional public finance. However, while we know that Treasury officials, and indeed Churchill, read and used Hawtrey's *Economica* article of 1925 to support their argument in 1929 that Lloyd George had an inflationary purpose behind his public works proposals (Clarke, 1988, pp. 53, 63), it would be a logical fallacy to argue that they took the view they did in 1929 *because* of Hawtrey's article. The Treasury had, after all, opposed Lloyd George's ideas about borrowing for public works, so as to reduce unemployment, in 1921 (Peden, 1993; Skidelsky, 1981). *Post hoc, ergo propter hoc* is bad logic, but *pre hoc, ergo non propter hoc* is sound enough.

It is difficult to trace the intellectual origins of Treasury thinking. Officials were primarily concerned with advising ministers, and did not normally quote academic authorities. For example, the only such authority referred to in Churchill's 'Treasury view' speech in 1929, and again in a White Paper (HMSO, 1929) which amplified his argument, was a work of economic history, first published in 1903, Archdeacon Cunningham's *The Growth of English Industry and Commerce in Modern Times*. The reference was concerned with the experience of the depression of 1847, which, according to Cunningham, was caused by over-investment in railways. Cunningham noted how a railway under construction diverted capital from other branches of industry and produced no immediate productive return, whereas the employment created by its construction raised imports and turned the exchanges against sterling (Cunningham, 1917, pp. 826–8). Cunningham himself quoted extensively from the analysis of James Wilson, *Capital, Currency and Banking*, which was based on articles published in the *Economist* in 1845 and 1847, and may fairly be said to be describing a traditional City view of the functioning of capital markets. Prior to the 1930s, Treasury officials had little direct contact with professional economists. On the other hand, Montagu Norman, the governor of the Bank of England, made it his business to make sure that the Chancellor and senior officials were acquainted with the City's views, by making frequent visits to the Treasury, and the Treasury was much more likely to consult City men than academic economists on questions relating to monetary policy.[1]

HAWTREY'S VIEWS

Hawtrey was the Treasury's main point of contact with professional economists in the 1920s. In 1919 he was released from routine administration by being appointed Director of the Treasury's Financial Enquiries Branch. The Financial Enquiries Branch amounted to no more than a little room inhabited by Hawtrey and an assistant, but, although Treasury officials would ask for Hawtrey's advice from time to time, there was no pressure of business and he was free to contemplate problems of economics and to write books on the subject. His books were taken seriously by professional economists; indeed, Keynes hailed Hawtrey's *Currency and Credit*, when it appeared in 1919 as 'one of the most original and profound treatises on the theory of money which has appeared for many years' (Keynes, 1920), and it was widely used as a textbook in the 1920s.[2] Although Hawtrey's influence on Treasury economic thinking is said to have waned in the 1930s, as senior Treasury officials encountered professional economists in person on the Economic Advisory Council's Committee on Economic Information (Howson, 1985; Howson and Winch, 1977), one of the most senior Treasury officials advising on financial policy, Sir Frederick Phillips, could still say in 1937 that Hawtrey understood professional economists in a way that he did not, so that as well as giving advice on his own account Hawtrey made intelligible what other economists were advising (Peden, 1979, p. 23).

Despite his reputation as an economist, Hawtrey appears to have developed his crowding out theory somewhat in isolation from the mainstream of economic thought (Deutscher, 1990). Although he counted Keynes as a friend from before 1914, and corresponded with other economists in the interwar period, including Pigou, Robertson and Hayek, and was elected as honorary secretary of the Royal Economic Society in 1937, Hawtrey approached economics from the point of view of a Treasury official. He only once held an academic appointment, in 1928–9, when he went on leave for a year to teach at Harvard. He had studied mathematics at Cambridge, where he was nineteenth Wrangler in his year, but he had scored low marks in the political economy paper in the Civil Service examination in 1903, having crammed the subject by attending lectures. He later recalled that J.H. Clapham, the economic historian, had been the first person to instruct him in economics, and Clapham's influence may be seen in the way in which Hawtrey tended to elucidate a subject by concrete historical examples as well as by theoretical analysis. The Edwardian Treasury did not provide a forum in which Hawtrey could debate theoretical issues: indeed, Hawtrey recalled that at the time he entered the Treasury, in 1904, officials were not generally interested in economics, which was not regarded as more important to their work than, say, a knowledge of local government (Hawtrey, 1966). What Hawtrey picked up in the Treasury before 1914, particularly from Sir John Bradbury, the Joint Permanent Secretary dealing with finance, was City and Bank of England views, as represented by Walter Bagehot, on the behaviour of financial markets and the efficacy of Bank rate in managing these markets. In *Lombard Street*, Bagehot criticized political economy of the period in which he wrote (c. 1870) for its neglect of time in its analysis of trade, and described how the supply of 'borrowable' money did not always match opportunities for investment. Moreover, for Bagehot the supply of loanable funds was not fixed, for he described how funds flowed in from abroad, when interest rates rose (1910, pp. 5, 48, 126, 133, 155–8).

Hawtrey's interest in economics went back to his schooldays at Eton, when he had read a number of works on the subject, including Mill's *Principles of Political Economy* (1848). Nevertheless, there is evidence that he was less than wholly conversant with the literature when he wrote his own first book, *Good and Bad Trade*, which was published in 1913. The only reference to another economist in the book was to Irving Fisher, and that reference was added after Hawtrey had finished the first draft. Moreover, although *Good and Bad Trade* was an analysis of the trade cycle, Hawtrey denied that his theory was derived from that of Alfred Marshall (Deutscher, 1990, pp. 8, 247). Presumably, in the course of writing the ten books that he published in the interwar period, Hawtrey became more familiar with the literature. Nevertheless, the position he adopted in 1913, that is to say the one derived from the City via Bradbury, was still recognizable in his *Century of Bank Rate*, published in 1938. As Hawtrey told Keynes in 1937: 'I have adhered to my fundamental ideas since 1913' (Keynes, 1973b, p. 55). *Good and Bad Trade* differed from previous analyses of the trade cycle by emphasizing monetary factors, rather than variations in harvests, the impact of inventions, or swings in speculative moods. Pigou, indeed, criticized Hawtrey for implying that the causes of trade fluctuations were exclusively monetary in origin (Pigou,

1913). It would be wrong therefore to see Hawtrey as merely adopting or expressing 'orthodox' views of pre-1914 economists.

In particular, as Deutscher (1990, pp. 36–8) has shown, Hawtrey was at best lukewarm in his response to the quantity theory of money. He was critical of Fisher's formalization of the relationship between the quantity of money in circulation (M), the velocity or rate of turnover of that money (V), the general level of prices (P), and the total number of transactions (T), as $MV = PT$. Hawtrey argued in the 1919 edition of *Currency and Credit* that the quantity theory was limited to comparing equilibrium positions, and that changes in the quantity of money did not cause proportionate changes in prices, because an initial change would bring about changes in other factors, whereas one of the conditions of the theory was that all other factors be held constant. Hawtrey generally insisted that monetary policy worked through interest rates directly, particularly on traders' willingness to hold stocks on credit, and not through changes in the quantity of money.

With regard to government borrowing crowding out private investment, Hawtrey's views were originally expressed in 1913 in *Good and Bad Trade*. The Minority Report of the Royal Commission on the Poor Laws had recommended in 1909 that there should be public investment in useful, but commercially unprofitable, works such as land-reclamation and forestry. Such works would be concentrated in years when the demand for labour was low, so as to stabilize employment and to take advantage of low interest rates. Hawtrey commented that:

> The writers of the Minority Report appear to have overlooked the fact that the Government by the very act of borrowing for this expenditure is withdrawing from the investment market saving which would otherwise be applied to the creation of capital.

Hawtrey believed that money which was saved would be spent 'sooner or later' on fixed capital or invested abroad. Government expenditure would thus, in his view, merely divert the demand for labour, either from industries that were concerned with the construction of fixed capital or industries that relied upon export markets. There was an assumption here, common enough at the time, that overseas investment stimulated demand for British exports, an assumption still held by the Treasury in 1929 (Hawtrey, 1913, pp. 260–1; HMSO, 1929, pp. 51–2).

Hawtrey's 1913 version of the 'Treasury view' could be seen as merely echoing the doctrines of classical economists, such as Adam Smith – 'what is annually saved is as regularly consumed as what is annually spent' – or David Ricardo – 'to save is to spend' – (Corry, 1958, pp. 38, 41). Indeed, Pigou, reviewing *Good and Bad Trade*, described Hawtrey's crowding out hypothesis as 'a fallacy' (Pigou, 1913) that he believed he had dealt with in his own

Wealth and Welfare (1912), in which he had supported the counter-cyclical proposals of the Minority Report. Even so, in his *Economica* article in 1925, Hawtrey defended his position with a deductive argument that was more subtle than that of the classical economists. He started with the condition that government borrowing was to be from the 'genuine savings' of the non-bank public, and not from the banks or people who had borrowed from banks. Within that constraint, he argued, government could attract idle balances held by the non-bank public by issuing a gilt-edged loan, but normally expenditure from the loan would be at the expense of future expenditure by the private sector. Hawtrey believed that the public as a whole would always keep an unspent margin of its income in the form of cash balances, and that therefore an increase in the investing public's holdings of government issues must, on his initial condition relating to 'genuine savings', normally lead to an equal diminution in other capital issues. He believed that the unspent margin would vary as a proportion of the public's income according to changes in the velocity of circulation of money, but that it was only when business confidence was exceptionally low that a gilt-edged loan could increase the velocity of circulation by attracting idle balances – unless one relaxed the condition that borrowing was not to involve an expansion of bank credit.

If the government did borrow from the banks, or from people who financed purchases of gilt-edged stock by borrowing from banks, matters would be different. Then government borrowing would create the bank credits that would enable the public to maintain their cash balances and the investment market to carry a greater amount of securities, and consequently loan-financed public works would give additional employment. However, as already noted, Hawtrey believed that expenditure on public works was unnecessary, the expansion of credit alone being sufficient to stimulate the economy, provided business showed a normal degree of enterprise. In his view, government borrowing would have the same effect if it were to meet a budget deficit arising from tax cuts, but, with due respect to prevailing rules of public finance (see below), he did not advocate such a course of action.

In his article, Hawtrey did concede that loan-financed public works might be necessary if business did not respond to a reduction in Bank rate to 2 per cent, as in the depression in 1894–96. However, in the second half of the 1920s, when the Bank of England and the Treasury gave priority to defending sterling's newly restored gold exchange value of $4.86, Bank rate ranged between 4 and 6.5 per cent (Howson, 1975; Moggridge, 1972), and the responsiveness of business to low interest rates was as yet unknown. More significantly, in the context of the late 1920s, Hawtrey believed that it would be possible to finance public works in Britain by diverting funds that would otherwise have gone into overseas investment. If sterling's exchange rate remained unchanged, the extra funds would lead to an expansion of credit, and therefore of employment, albeit at the expense of investment and employment in other countries. He thought that it was remarkable that advocates of public expenditure as a remedy for unemployment never seemed to consider drawing upon the international investment market (Hawtrey, 1925, p. 46). In the event, diversion of funds from overseas to home investment came to play a major part in Keynes's arguments in support of public works (Keynes, 1972, pp. 115–21; Keynes, 1981a, pp. 221–3, 807, 811).

PUBLIC FINANCE AND ECONOMIC THEORY

In order to understand the impact of economic theory on policy it is necessary to understand the framework of public finance within which policy would have to be implemented. Interwar Treasury officials tried to maintain the tradition, established by Sir Robert Peel and William Gladstone between the 1840s and the 1860s, of an impartial state, standing apart from competing economic interests. The three key characteristics of this tradition were: first, the balanced budget convention, ensuring that any attempt by politicians to buy popularity through public expenditure would be offset by the odium incurred by raising taxes. Second, the gold standard, whereby sterling had a fixed value in terms of gold, and therefore with all other currencies that were also on the gold standard, ensuring a considerable degree of independence for the Bank of England from political pressures. And third, free trade, which ensured that no group of producers could bargain for political favours. Both the gold standard and free trade acted to maintain Britain as an open economy, and it was generally believed in the Treasury that, if British industry encountered competition in home as well as in international markets, it would maintain a competitive edge in both.

The gold standard had been largely in suspense during World War I, and was formally suspended in the spring of 1919. However, a return to gold was the object of Treasury policy from that year until it was achieved under Churchill's chancellorship in 1925, and it was only as a result of overwhelming international speculation against sterling that the gold standard was to be suspended in September 1931. The Conservative party, which was in power for most of the interwar period, favoured tariffs, but an electoral reverse in 1923 on this question had induced a sense of caution in the party leadership. Indeed Churchill, only recently restored to the Conservative party whip before being appointed as chancellor in 1924, was as committed to free trade in principle as his officials, at least down to the post-1929 depression. Thereafter the need to curb Britain's balance of payments deficit in 1931, and to prevent a free fall by sterling after the suspension of the gold standard, provided strong arguments in favour of a general tariff, which was adopted in 1932, when Neville Chamberlain was chancellor.

The demise of the gold standard and free trade in 1931–32 can only have strengthened the Treasury's determination to maintain the doctrine of balanced budgets, although the difficulties of balancing the budget during the depression, and later during the period of rearmament on the eve of the war, led to a good deal of fiscal 'window dressing' (Middleton, 1985). However, most public works were financed outside the budget as then conventionally defined (the chancellor's budget being solely concerned with accounting to Parliament for central government revenue and central government expenditure). Parliament did authorize central government borrowing for specific purposes: for example, investment by the Post Office, then a government department, in telephone lines. However, the rule for central government borrowing, as maintained by the Treasury as late as 1935, was that the money return on such investment should be sufficient to pay off both capital and interest on the loan (Peden, 1979, p. 72). There was no published figure for a public sector borrowing requirement, and subject to central government supervision, local authorities (which were chiefly responsible for roads as well as public sector housing) and public utilities, such as the Central Electricity Board, which was responsible for the rapidly expanding national electricity grid, raised loans outside the chancellor's budget, albeit usually with a government guarantee.

What was at question in 1929, therefore, was not whether there should be a budget deficit, but rather what would be the effects of public sector borrowing outside the chancellor's budget. Lloyd George had made what was essentially an electioneering pledge to abolish 'abnormal' unemployment by sharply increasing loan expenditure on public works over the next two years, without inflation, and while maintaining the gold standard and free trade (Liberal Party, 1929, p. 62). Treasury officials had good reason to suspect Lloyd George's commitment to sound finance: only eight years earlier, while still prime minister, he had considered a deliberate policy of inflation as a means of reducing unemployment (Peden, 1993), and Bradbury had probably had Lloyd George in mind when, in a famous phrase, he described the gold standard in 1925 as 'knave proof' (Grigg, 1948, p. 183). Treasury officials, as guardians of orthodox public finance, were unlikely to look at economic theories, including Hawtrey's, in isolation from politics, especially when Lloyd George was associated with a particular proposal for public expenditure. It is true, of course, that the Treasury's views rested on an implicit model of the economy, in which factors of production, unshielded from international competition, were flexible, in contrast to fixed principles of public finance, but most Treasury officials on the finance side of the Treasury were more familiar with public finance than they were with economics (Clarke, 1990).

One problem facing Treasury officials in drafting their arguments in early 1929 was that Hawtrey was away in Harvard at the time. The most important officials who had to advise Churchill were Sir Richard Hopkins, the controller of the Treasury's finance and supply services departments, who was responsible for financial policy and control of public expenditure; F.W. Leith-Ross, his deputy in the finance department, and P.J. Grigg, the chancellor's principal private secretary. None of them had formal training in economics, apart from any preparation they might have done for the economics paper for the Civil Service examination. Hopkins had studied classics in part I of the tripos at Cambridge, and history in part II, with first-class honours in both. He had been chairman of the Board of Inland Revenue before moving to the Treasury in 1927, and certainly had a firm grasp of public finance, but it was apparently only after he went to the Treasury that he read a wide range of works in economics (Peden, 1983). Leith-Ross had got a first in both Mods and Greats in *Literae Humaniores* at Oxford, and had served in the Treasury since 1909. Although he was to be given the title of chief economic adviser to His Majesty's Government in 1932, Leith-Ross had learned most of what he knew about financial policy while working on reparation questions after World War I. He himself admitted that the title as chief economic adviser was a misnomer, most of his work in that post being concerned with economic diplomacy (Leith-Ross, 1968, pp. 145–6). Treasury papers suggest that Leith-Ross looked to Hawtrey for economic advice, but that he did not always accept it. Grigg had taken first-class honours in mathematics in both parts of the Cambridge tripos, and had entered the Treasury in 1913. As private secretary to successive chancellors from 1921, Grigg had considerable experience in helping to draw up a balanced budget, which may help to explain why he could never see in Keynes's various proposals for public works, tariffs or devaluation 'anything but different manifestations of a thesis that nations, unlike private individuals, can live so as both to have their cake and eat it' (Grigg, 1948, p. 257). Adam Smith could not have put the point more succinctly.

It is probable that Hopkins, Leith-Ross and Grigg had all at some time read *The Wealth of Nations*, and were familiar with the final chapter on the want of parsimony in government, in peace as well as in war (Smith, 1904). World War I had certainly dramatically increased the burden of the national debt on the chancellor's budget, and, contrary to the generally accepted view that interwar public expenditure was rigidly constrained by Treasury parsimony, the elasticity of expenditure growth relative to GDP growth (measured at current prices) was higher in the period 1924–37 than it was to be in 1960–76, although the latter period is generally accepted as being one of rapid growth in public expenditure (Middleton, 1982, p. 50). In these circumstances, Treasury officials may well have been more concerned to maintain traditional rules of public finance that curbed the state's propensity to spend than they were with economic theory.

THE TREASURY VIEW OF 1929

It would seem to have been in this spirit that Leith-Ross and Grigg turned in 1929 to Hawtrey's (1925) article in *Economica* (which Grigg described as being of 'extreme obscurity').[3] Clarke (1988) has carefully pieced together the story of how the Treasury view emerged, and I depart from his account only in emphasizing the extent to which the Treasury view in 1929 did *not* accurately reflect Hawtrey's views.

It was known that Lloyd George was soon to launch an initiative on unemployment in what would be an election year. In February, some Conservative ministers were sufficiently concerned about their party's prospects to discuss in Cabinet the advisability of stealing the Liberal leader's thunder, either by raising a government-guaranteed loan for public works in the British Empire (to encourage exports and emigration) or by building roads at home. The Treasury view of 1929 was thus originally formulated for use by Churchill in Cabinet, that draft being prepared by Hopkins's most senior subordinate in the supply services department, Gilbert Upcott, indicating that the question was seen as partly being about the control of public expenditure, as well as by Leith-Ross's principal subordinate dealing with financial policy, Frederick Phillips.

The Cabinet was told in February 1929 that 'unless the Government are prepared to take steps to bring about an inflation of banking credits', public expenditure could only create employment if the government could find ways of spending money that would create more employment than private enterprise would with the same money (PRO, 1929b). In March, after Lloyd George had launched his programme, Churchill asked his officials what would happen if £100 million of new credit were created by government borrowing from the Bank of England on ways and means. Leith-Ross replied that the result would be to increase prices in Britain, thereby encouraging imports and production for the home market, but discouraging exports. Some of the extra credit would be used for purchasing shares on the then booming New York Stock Exchange. With the sterling–dollar exchange already hovering about the level at which it would be profitable to export gold from London, the Bank of England would then have to protect its reserves by raising the bank rate, as it had already done the previous month, from $4^{1}/_{2}$ to $5^{1}/_{2}$ per cent, until 'the expansion of credit (and the improvement of industry) that had occurred had been nullified. We should therefore soon be precisely where we were, except that we should have lost some gold'. It might be

possible to defer an increase in Bank rate by increasing the fiduciary issue –
the amount of notes unbacked by gold that the Bank of England was allowed
to issue under the Currency and Bank Notes Act 1928 – thereby releasing
gold for supporting the exchange rate, but Hopkins thought that such action
would frighten foreign holders of sterling into withdrawing their balances
from London.[4] 'Inflation' was thus held to be incompatible with maintenance
of the gold standard.

When Lloyd George's claims appeared in print in the middle of March as a
pamphlet, *We Can Conquer Unemployment* (Liberal Party 1929), Churchill
advocated the publication of a rebuttal. The latter appeared in May, shortly
before the election, in the form of a White Paper incorporating comments by
the ministries of Labour, Transport and Health, and the Post Office, as well as
by the Treasury, on the Liberal proposals (HMSO, 1929). The general drift of
the White Paper was that the Liberal schemes were impracticable in the time
allotted to them, and that they would not provide as much employment as was
claimed. The Treasury's contribution developed arguments drafted earlier for
Churchill's use in Cabinet and in his budget speech. The Liberal proposals
were costed at £125 million in each of the next two years, compared with
actual provision of £254 million for state capital expenditure in the previous
four years. It was noted that the Liberal pamphlet claimed that the necessary
funds could be raised from idle savings or by diverting money from overseas
investment. The Treasury conceded that not all savings were currently being
invested, but argued that most balances that had accumulated in the banks
were funds that firms wished to keep liquid while business was slack, and
which were not, therefore, available for the long-term borrowing necessary to
finance capital expenditure by the state. As for overseas investment, the
Treasury doubted whether the kind of controls that had been applied to
capital movements during World War I could be applied in peace, and noted
that an attempt to divert overseas investment by competing with high interest
rates in New York would force up rates in Britain. In these circumstances, the
Treasury concluded, 'a very large proportion of any additional Government
borrowings' could only be financed, 'without inflation', by diverting money
which would otherwise have been used 'soon' by industry at home. The
Treasury's preferred solution was for private enterprise to improve its efficiency and to adjust to changes in demand (HMSO, 1929).

It will be noticed that the Treasury view of 1929 took little or no account of
the last part of Hawtrey's article in *Economica* (1925), that is his belief that a
government loan could raise money from the international investment market
rather than from funds available for home investment. Hawtrey had argued
that such an operation would be the equivalent of the importation of capital,
which, under the gold standard, would bring about an expansion of credit.
However, Hawtrey had admitted that in a highly industrialized country, where

both import and export trades were sensitive to price movements, the effect of credit expansion would be to increase imports more than it increased employment (Hawtrey, 1925, p. 46), and it is understandable if Treasury officials felt that there was little of practical value in the suggestion.

On his return from Harvard, however, Hawtrey expanded on his theory relating to the import of capital. In two memoranda[5] in June he argued that the only obstacle to an expansion of credit was the loss of gold that would ensue. The threat to the gold standard could be avoided if the government borrowed funds that would otherwise have gone into overseas investment, or if the government borrowed gold or foreign exchange abroad. Contrary to Leith-Ross's assumption that the effects of credit expansion would quickly be cancelled by the operation of the gold standard, Hawtrey now argued, that, while part of the resulting credit expansion would raise demand for imports, part would raise demand for home-produced goods for which there was no foreign substitute, thereby raising national income and employment. Hawtrey still regarded public works as an unnecessarily complicated way of achieving what could be achieved by monetary policy acting as a stimulus to private investment, but he was willing to see public works and monetary policy acting in tandem. His favoured monetary policy was for the government to raise a loan on the London market and to apply the proceeds to paying off Treasury bills. The loan, he believed would absorb 'investible savings' that would otherwise have gone abroad, while the reduction in Treasury bills would force the banks to find other outlets for their funds, in the form of commercial bills or advances to traders. Clarke (1988, p. 145) has commented that Hawtrey was being consistent in specifying the conditions under which 'crowding out' took place, and that Hawtrey was not certain that these conditions prevailed when there were unemployed resources. In the 1928 edition of *Currency and Credit*, Hawtrey had written that a rise in prices and an increase in production were 'to a great extent, *alternatives*' (original emphasis).

To judge from his marginal comments on Hawtrey's memorandum dealing with debt policy and unemployment, Hopkins was not impressed by the applicability of Hawtrey's ideas to the real world. In particular, he felt that the main practical objection to the funding of Treasury bills would be that the gilt-edged market was not in a very favourable condition, and the $4^1/2$ per cent stock that Hawtrey contemplated could only be sold at a discount. Hopkins certainly felt no need to pursue Hawtrey's idea urgently. It was not until October that he secured comment on it from Sir Otto Niemeyer, his predecessor as controller of the Treasury's finance department, and now a leading figure at the Bank of England. Niemeyer thought Hawtrey's ideas were 'very odd', and pointed to the practical objection that the banks could not find alternative short-term investments to Treasury bills, such as commercial bills, on the scale that Hawtrey contemplated (PRO, 1929c, ff. 78, 79). It is difficult to avoid the conclusion that Hawtrey's importance in the formulation of the Treasury view can easily be exaggerated.

Treasury officials liked to think of themselves as practical men, as opposed to professional economists, whom they intended to see as abstract theorists. Regarding their own sphere of public finance, they saw themselves as maintaining the credit of the British state, in the sense that historically it had been able to raise loans on international money markets at lower rates of interest than had many foreign governments. All would have been familiar with the dictum of what, in their formative years at the Treasury, had been the leading academic study of public finance that: 'a nation cannot, any more than an individual, keep adding continuously to its liabilities without coming to the end of its resources' (Bastable, 1892, p. 581). The nation's resources, in this context, meant its taxable capacity, for it was from tax receipts, plus any money return from state capital investment, that the interest on loans for public works would have to be paid. Hence officials' belief that loans had to be seen by money markets to be for productive purposes. In looking for the likely reactions of money markets, Treasury officials, like the Bank of England, were disposed to be guided by what was happening in the market rather than by estimates of national savings or overseas investment. For example, they believed that the tendency of capital movements could only be gauged by discount rates in the money market, and by pressure on the exchange rate (HMSO, 1929, pp. 47–8). As it happened, the debate in 1929 on the Treasury view coincided with pressure on sterling brought about by the movement of funds to New York to join in stock exchange speculation there.

THE TREASURY VIEW IN THE 1930s

The terms of the debate were quickly changed. The general election of June 1929 resulted in the formation of a minority Labour government with a commitment to doing something about unemployment. By June 1930 the government had approved public works schemes totalling £110.1 million, of which, however, only £44.3 million had started, owing to the inevitable delays in planning and implementing road works and the like (Middleton, 1983, p. 361). However, the minister responsible for unemployment policy, J.H. Thomas, the Lord Privy Seal, was at one with the Treasury in believing that the fundamental problem lay with the export trades, and the schemes he favoured were those designed to lower costs rather than to provide relief for the unemployed. He agreed with the Chancellor of the Exchequer, Philip Snowden, that there was to be no 'inflation', no subsidies to inefficient industries, and no interference with free trade. Consequently, Snowden had no difficulty in persuading the Cabinet not to adopt ambitious public works schemes put forward in 1930 by Thomas's junior colleague, Oswald Mosley, the chancellor of the Duchy of Lancaster (Skidelsky, 1975, pp. 180–2, 192–210).

Meanwhile, the Macmillan Committee on Finance and Industry had been set up to inquire into how the banking system affected the economy, giving Keynes, who was a member of the committee, the chance to engage in debate on the Treasury view with Hopkins, who was a witness. Hawtrey had appeared earlier as a witness, and had put to the committee his ideas on diverting overseas investment, so as to strengthen Britain's reserves and make possible an expansion of credit, but significantly Hawtrey appeared in a personal capacity, and it was made clear that he did not speak for the Treasury. Hopkins took exceptional care in preparing the Treasury's official evidence, consulting Niemeyer as well as Leith-Ross, Phillips and Hawtrey. As Clarke (1988, pp. 148–56) has shown, Hopkins retreated from the Treasury view of 1929 in so far as it related to the supply of loanable funds, and avoided debating the theoretical aspects of Keynes's ideas. Hopkins conceded that, on Keynes's assumptions, public works that did not produce a money return sufficient to pay the capital and interest on a loan might still pay for themselves partly by diverting capital from abroad, partly by mobilizing idle balances, partly by diminishing the cost of unemployment relief, and partly by increased revenue arising from increased economic activity, but he doubted if these effects could be calculated. He took his stand on the practical objections that the 1929 White Paper had raised to a rapid expansion of public works. In particular, he pointed out that, if a large public works programme seemed to investors to be wasteful, financial markets would expect the value of government stock to fall, and investors would turn to overseas issues, thereby increasing pressure on the exchange rate, which in turn would lead to a rise in Bank rate (Keynes, 1981b, pp. 166–79). Crowding out, in other words, would occur because of the way in which money markets would perceive loan-financed public works, not because of the rights and wrongs of abstract theory.

Keynes's theoretical position became more sophisticated from 1931, with the development of the concept of the multiplier. In 1933, in *The Means to Prosperity*, he advocated a reduction in taxation and an increase in loan-financed public works, predicting that the chancellor's budget would benefit after a time lag, as national income rose (Keynes, 1972, pp. 335–66). Once more, Treasury officials met theory with public finance. Hopkins pointed out that the lag between income being earned and tax being paid was, on average, 20 months in the case of income tax, and 32 months in the case of surtax (the tax then paid on higher incomes), and during this period the budget would remain unbalanced. Phillips, who had replaced Leith-Ross as Hopkins's principal subordinate on the finance side of the Treasury, noted: 'it is no good saying that the works will produce the savings for investment, for *ex hypothesi* the borrowing precedes the works' (PRO, 1933).[6] In this case, after prolonged debate with his Cambridge colleague, Dennis Robertson, Keynes had to admit that the Treasury was right, and that 'dishoarding' (i.e. the mobilization of idle savings) and credit expansion were a necessary preparation for the process, described in the *General Theory*, whereby increased investment was accompanied by increased savings. Without that preparation 'congestion of the capital market', i.e. crowding out, would occur (Middleton, 1985, pp. 167–8). In practical terms, relating to the need to expand credit, this brought one back to a position not very far from Hawtrey's in 1925, but the Treasury continued to pursue a cautious monetary policy, funding debt as opportunity occurred (Howson, 1975).

Hawtrey had thought that loan-financed public works might be necessary as an employment policy if private investment did not respond to a fall in Bank rate to 2 per cent. Such a fall occurred in 1932, and Bank rate stayed at 2 per cent until the eve of war in 1939. Nevertheless, Treasury officials continued to believe that public works as a remedy for unemployment were in themselves quite futile. In 1935, when Lloyd George was again pressing loan-financed public works as an employment policy, Treasury advice was that an expansion of borrowing by local authorities would be useful for keeping up the impetus of recovery from the slump, and in 1937 Phillips endorsed plans for the creation of a reserve of public works for use in the next depression. However, he also advised that any programme of public works that forced government to borrow repeatedly in the market 'might give rise to serious apprehension as to the state of the national finances'. Such apprehension would make it difficult for the Bank of England 'to produce that lowering of the rate of interest which must always remain the principal weapon in the hands of the authorities during times of trade depression' (Peden, 1984, pp. 176–8). This opinion was very much in line with Hawtrey's *Century of Bank Rate*.

The need to rearm against Germany forced the Treasury to accept large-scale loan-financed expenditure from 1937, helping to offset the effects of the recession in 1938. Even so, Phillips, writing in April 1939, stated only that unemployment '*probably* would have been worse' than it actually was without rearmament, and advised concerning statements in Parliament about borrowing and inflation:

> I agree with Mr Hawtrey that the real stimulus comes from reflationary finance. If there were no reflationary finance, the government works would tend merely to replace private works without much effect on employment. But this is the famous or infamous 'Treasury view', still a most bitter subject of controversy which it would be a great mistake to raise. (Peden, 1980, p. 6).

Treasury officials had learned to talk about 'reflationary finance' rather than 'inflationary finance', and to be cautious about public controversy about economic theory. However, the Treasury view was still to be found in Whitehall as the interwar period drew to a close.

CONCLUSION

To return to my original questions: it would seem that the connection between the Treasury view and the doctrines of professional economists was an indirect one. Hawtrey himself had developed his ideas in 1913 somewhat in isolation from professional economists, and few professional economists subscribed to them in the interwar period. His ideas were used by the Treasury only in so far as they were in accordance with the traditions of public finance. Indeed, this chapter raises the question of whether the history of economic thought should be confined to the history of the ideas of professional economists, or whether it should be extended to economic ideas to be found in the City and Whitehall. Hawtrey himself appears to have absorbed City views via Bradbury, and Treasury officials in general were more likely to be concerned with the views of the City than they were with economic theory. In 1930, Hopkins distanced himself from the theory associated with the Treasury view of the previous year, without, however, abandoning objections to loan-financed public works based on administrative practicalities and the likely reactions on money markets. As late as 1939, the thinking underlying the deficit financing of rearmament, and its impact on unemployment, owed more to Hawtrey than to Keynes, and was not fundamentally different from the thinking that had underlain the Treasury view ten years earlier.

Professor Corry (Chapter 1, pp. 1–2) has drawn our attention to the danger of ambiguity in terms such as unemployment. The same danger is present in our ideas about the functions of institutions, which change over time. Interwar Treasury officials would have agreed with Nigel Lawson that 'the promotion of jobs and employment is not the Treasury's principal responsibility' (see Chapter 5, p. 93). Their responsibility was maintenance of sound finance, rather than of management of the economy as a whole, and it was not until 1944 that government came to accept maintenance of a high and stable level of employment as one of its responsibilities. Even then, Treasury officials incorporated passages designed to protect sound finance in the White Paper on *Employment Policy* (HMSO, 1944).

NOTES

1. For example, the decision in principle to return to the gold standard was taken in 1919 on the advice of the Cunliffe Committee, which had 11 bankers but only one academic economist (Pigou) on it. The decision to return in 1925 was largely taken on the advice of the Chamberlain-Bradbury Committee, on which Pigou was again the only economist, with the other experts being a Treasury official, a former Treasury official, and a partner in Baring Brothers (Boyce, 1987, pp. 31, 66).
2. David Laidler has suggested that Hawtrey influenced the monetary explanation of cyclical fluctuations developed at Harvard and Chicago in the interwar period (Laidler 1993).
3. PRO (1929a), Grigg to Churchill, 2 March.
4. PRO (1929a), Leith-Ross to Churchill, 12 March.
5. PRO (1929c), 'The Liberal unemployment plan', 13 June; and 'Debt policy and unemployment', 29 June.
6. PRO (1933), note by Hopkins, 13 March; and 'Questions for Keynes', 20 March.

REFERENCES

Bagehot, W. (1910), *Lombard Street: A Description of the Money Market*, new edition with introduction by Hartley Withers, London: Smith, Elder and Co. First published 1873.

Bastable, C.F. (1892), *Public Finance*, London: Macmillan.

Boyce, R. (1987), *British Capitalism at the Crossroads 1919–1932: A Study in Politics, Economics, and International Relations*, Cambridge: Cambridge University Press.

Casson, M. (1983), *Economics of Unemployment: An Historical Perspective*, Oxford: Martin Robertson.

Clarke, P. (1988), *The Keynesian Revolution in the Making, 1924–1936*, Oxford: Clarendon Press.

Clarke, P. (1990), 'The Treasury's analytical model of the British economy between the wars', in M.O. Furner and B. Supple (eds), *The State and Economic Knowledge: The American and British Experiences*, Cambridge: Cambridge University Press, 171–207.

Corry, B.A. (1958), 'The theory of the economic effects of government expenditure in the English classical economy', *Economica*, new series, **25** (97), February, 34–48.

Cunningham, W. (1917), *The Growth of English Industry and Commerce in Modern Times*, vol. 2, *Laissez Faire*, Cambridge: Cambridge University Press. First published 1903.

Deutscher, P. (1990), *R.G. Hawtrey and the Development of Macroeconomics*, London: Macmillan.

Grigg, P.J. (1948), *Prejudice and Judgment*, London: Jonathan Cape.

Hansard (1906), H.C. Deb., fourth series, vol. 156, col. 290.

Hansard (1929), H.C. Deb., fifth series, vol. 227, cols 53–6.

Hawtrey, R.G. (1913), *Good and Bad Trade: An Analysis into the Causes of Trade Fluctuations*, London: Constable & Co.

Hawtrey, R.G. (1919), *Currency and Credit*, London: Longmans, Green & Co. Second edition 1923; third 1928; fourth 1950.

Hawtrey, R.G. (1925), 'Public expenditure and the demand for labour', *Economica*, **5** (13), March, 38–48.

Hawtrey, R.G. (1938), *A Century of Bank Rate*, London: Longmans, Green & Co. Second edition 1962.

Hawtrey, R.G. (1966), Taped conversation between Sir Ralph Hawtrey and Sir Alec Cairncross, Hawtrey papers, Churchill College, Cambridge, file 13/5.

HMSO (1929), *Memoranda on Certain Proposals Relating to Unemployment*, Cmnd 3331, parliamentary papers 1928–29, vol. xvi.

HMSO (1944), *Employment Policy*, Cmnd 6527, parliamentary papers, vol. viii.

Howson, S. (1975), *Domestic Monetary Management in Britain 1919–38*, Cambridge: Cambridge University Press.

Howson, S. (1985), 'Hawtrey and the real world', in G.C. Harcourt (ed.), *Keynes and his Contemporaries: The Sixth and Centennial Keynes Seminar held at the University of Kent at Canterbury, 1983*, London: Macmillan, 142–88.

Howson, S. and Winch, D. (1977), *The Economic Advisory Council, 1930–1939*, Cambridge: Cambridge University Press.

Keynes, J.M. (1920), Review of Hawtrey's *Currency and Credit* in *Economic Journal*, **30** (119), September, 362–5.

Keynes, J.M. (1972), *Collected Writings*: vol. 9, *Essays in Persuasion*, London: Macmillan.

Keynes, J.M. (1973a), *Collected Writings*: vol. 7, *The General Theory of Employment, Interest and Money*, London: Macmillan.

Keynes, J.M. (1973b), *Collected Writings*, vol. 14, *The General Theory and After*, Part II, *Defence and Development*, London: Macmillan.

Keynes, J.M. (1981a), *Collected Writings*: vol. 19 (Parts 1 and 2), *Activities 1922–1929: The Return to Gold and Industrial Policy*, London: Macmillan.

Keynes, J.M. (1981b), *Collected Writings*: vol. 20, *Activities 1929–1931: Rethinking Employment and Unemployment Policies*, London: Macmillan.

Laidler, D. (1993), 'Hawtrey, Harvard, and the origins of the Chicago tradition', *Journal of Political Economy*, **101** (6), December, 1068–1103.

Leith-Ross, Sir F. (1968), *Money Talks: Fifty Years of International Finance*, London: Hutchinson.

Liberal Party (1929), *We Can Conquer Unemployment*, London: Cassell.

Middleton, R. (1982), 'The Treasury in the 1930s: political and administrative constraints to acceptance of the "new" economics', *Oxford Economic Papers*, new series, **34** (1), March, 48–77.

Middleton, R. (1983), 'The Treasury and public investment: a perspective on interwar economic management', *Public Administration*, **61** (4), winter, 351–70.

Middleton, R. (1985), *Towards the Managed Economy: Keynes, the Treasury and the Fiscal Policy Debate of the 1930s*, London: Methuen.

Mill, J.S. (1848, 1966), *Principles of Political Economy*, in J. Robson (ed.), *Collected Works of John Stuart Mill*, University of Toronto Press (Routledge & Kegan Paul, vols 2 and 3).

Moggridge, D.E. (1972), *British Monetary Policy 1924–1931: The Norman Conquest of $4.86*, Cambridge: Cambridge University Press.

Moggridge, D.E. (1992), *Maynard Keynes: An Economist's Biography*, London: Routledge.

Peden, G.C. (1979), *British Rearmament and the Treasury 1932–1939*, Edinburgh: Scottish Academic Press.

Peden, G.C. (1980), 'Keynes, the Treasury and unemployment in the later 1930s', *Oxford Economic Papers*, new series, **32** (1), March, 1–18.

Peden, G.C. (1983), 'Sir Richard Hopkins and the "Keynesian revolution" in employ-ment policy, 1929–45', *Economic History Review*, **36**, May, 281–96.

Peden, G.C. (1984), 'The "Treasury view" on public works and employment in the interwar period', *Economic History Review*, **37**, May 167–81.

Peden, G.C. (1993), 'The road to and from Gairloch: Lloyd George, unemployment, inflation and the "Treasury view" in 1921', *Twentieth Century British History*, **4** (3), 224–49.

Pigou, A.C. (1912), *Wealth and Welfare*, London: Macmillan.

Pigou, A.C. (1913), Review of Hawtrey's *Good and Bad Trade* in *Economic Journal*, **23** (92), December, 580–84.

PRO (Public Record Office, London) (1929a), 'Cure for unemployment memoranda of 1928 and 1929', Treasury papers, series 172, file 2095.

PRO (Public Record Office, London) (1929b), Cabinet Paper 53 (29), 'Unemploy-ment', note prepared in the Treasury, 23 February, Cabinet Office papers, series 24, vol. 202.

PRO (Public Record Office, London) (1929c), 'Memoranda on the unemployment situation', Treasury papers, series 175, file 26.

PRO (Public Record Office, London) (1933), 'General monetary and financial policy', Treasury papers, series 175, file 17.

Skidelsky, R. (1975), *Oswald Mosley*, London: Macmillan.

Skidelsky, R. (1981), 'Keynes and the Treasury view: the case for and against an active unemployment policy, 1920–1929', in W.J. Mommsen (ed.), *The Emergence of the Welfare State in Britain and Germany, 1850–1950*, London: Croom Helm, 167–87.

Skidelsky, R. (1992), *John Maynard Keynes*, vol. 2, *The Economist as Saviour 1920–1937*, London: Macmillan.

Smith, A. (1904), *The Wealth of Nations*, edited by Edwin Cannan, 2 vols, London: Methuen. First published 1776.

Wilson, J. (1847), *Capital, Currency, and Banking*, London: Office of The Econo-mist.

Winch, D. (1969), *Economics and Policy: A Historical Study*, London: Hodder and Stoughton.

5. Unemployment policy since the war – the theory and the practice*

Alan Budd

In this chapter I seek to provide a history of unemployment policy since the war and to show how it was influenced by events and ideas. In particular I attempt to answer the following questions:

- What did the government do?
- Why did it do it?
- To what extent were its actions influenced by academic developments in economic thought?

The first two questions are rather easier to answer than the third. Politicians are not in the habit of citing academic authorities either when they introduce policies or when they write about them in their memoirs afterwards. (We may recall Keynes's apt comment on practical men and defunct academic scribblers.) My rather unsatisfactory solution to this problem is to provide a final section in which I attempt to relate policy changes to developments in economics while admitting the difficulty of establishing the direct link between them.

I start with a brief account of the events, the actions and the ideas. I then provide a more detailed account of the policy developments and the explanations provided for them.

A BRIEF HISTORY

Figures 5.1 to 5.3 summarize the record. The post-war period up to the late 1960s appears to be a golden age of low unemployment and modest inflation. Unemployment was however tending to rise and balance of payments prob-

*The views expressed in this chapter are those of the author and do not necessarily represent those of HM Treasury. I am most grateful to Charlie Bean and Bill Wells for comments on an earlier draft. I am also grateful to Matthew Hunt and Ian Walker for their help in tracking down sources.

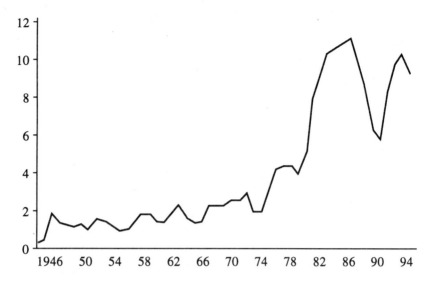

Source: 1944–61 Feinstein (1972); 1962–94 OECD

Figure 5.1   Registered unemployed as a percentage of total labour force

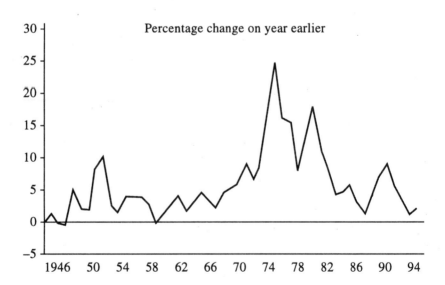

[1]Uses cost of living index 1944–47

Figure 5.2   RPI inflation[1]

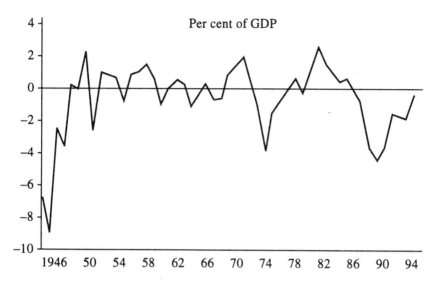

Per cent of GDP

Figure 5.3   Balance of payments current account

lems (which provided the main constraint on policy during this period) tended to occur at ever higher levels of unemployment. The 1970s saw inflation and unemployment scaling new heights. The 1980s and 1990s have seen inflation brought back down to the levels of the 1960s but unemployment has remained high.

The history of policy can be divided into two broad periods. The first which runs to the late 1970s (though 1976 was an important date on the way) saw unemployment primarily as a problem of demand. The government was committed to high employment and believed it had the means to deliver it. In fact unemployment stayed unexpectedly low without the need for direct fiscal reflation for nearly 15 years after the war, It was not until 1959 that a Budget was primarily directed at expanding demand in order to reduce unemployment. Until then (and for many years after) fiscal policy was directed mainly at avoiding problems of the balance of payments and/ or inflation, particularly the former. Temporary increases in unemployment were seen as an unfortunate side effect of the occasional need to tighten fiscal policy for balance of payments reasons. No one doubted that unemployment could be reduced by a fiscal expansion in the absence of balance of payments constraints. From the start it was recognized that a commitment to full employment increased the risk of high inflation. Thus there was a search for means to reduce that risk. A favoured solution was incomes policies of one sort or another in an attempt to combine low unemployment with low inflation.

The period of demand-management, with increasing reliance on incomes policies, lasted till the late 1970s. The emphasis on demand-management should not be taken to mean that there was no use of microeconomic policies directed at reducing unemployment in this period. In the immediate post-war period there was a challenge – successfully met – to reabsorb the returning troops. There was a large array of policies designed to reduce regional discrepancies in unemployment. There was also a general tendency, as the years passed, to move away from market solutions in the labour market as in other markets. This was most notably true under the Heath and Wilson and Callaghan governments (despite Mr Callaghan's speech of 1976). Given the loss of belief in market mechanisms it was not surprising that measures were taken – on the social security system, on redundancy arrangements, on union powers, etc. – which, with hindsight, can be seen as having unfavourable market consequences.

This loss of confidence in markets accompanied the view that combining low unemployment with low inflation was a matter of sensible bargaining between the government on the one hand and employers and unions on the other. Low unemployment and job security, together with adequate profits, could be offered as a reward for wage and price moderation. Microeconomic policies were designed to assist this process by equalizing employment opportunities throughout the country, for example through regional selective assistance, selective employment tax, the regional employment premium, etc. It was hoped that such policies would increase the effectiveness of demand-management by reducing the risk of inflation.

From the late 1970s emphasis shifted from seeing unemployment as primarily a demand problem to seeing it as a supply-side problem. All the emphasis since then has been on finding policies which would reduce structural unemployment by improving the operation of markets, particularly the labour market. In the particular case of the labour market there has been, in turn, trade union reform, changes in the social security system and concern with the specific conditions of the low paid and the long-term unemployed. One could summarize the history as moving from demand management to the supply side via incomes policies.

If one sought a similar encapsulation of the history of thought one might describe it as from Keynes to Friedman via Phillips. Since the classic paper by Friedman was published in 1968 one might think that the history has ended rather early. However, there was considerable delay before Friedman's insights were incorporated into economic policy and much of the consequent history of thought has really been a development of his ideas.

The relationship between academic thought and economic policy is, as I have said, difficult to establish but it is possible to think of policy-makers grappling with the question of defining and measuring the equilibrium level of unemployment. In practical terms the problem emerged as the apparent need for ever-higher levels of unemployment to maintain satisfactory conditions for the balance of payments and/or inflation. It was still believed that demand management could be used to reduce unemployment but its use was increasingly inhibited. Why was this happening?

There were a number of diagnoses. One class of explanation saw the problem primarily as one of 'cost-push inflation' which was validated by the commitment to full employment. The solution was incomes policies of one sort or another. A second type of explanation saw the problem primarily as one of economic performance. Hence the search for ways of increasing the underlying growth of the economy in the hope that it would again be possible to combine low unemployment with low inflation and a satisfactory balance of payments. Solutions included the establishment of the National Economic Development Office, Mr Maudling's 'dash for growth' and the National Plan. A third explanation focused on the exchange rate. The solutions included the devaluation of 1967 and the move to floating in 1972.

One could perhaps describe these policies as comprising 'augmented Keynesianism'. Sometime in the 1970s, and certainly by 1979, the policies were rejected because they had apparently failed. The crucial change was the belief that the problem lay in the supply conditions in the labour market. In terms of the history of thought, that change of emphasis can be linked to Friedman. It produced the analysis that the post-war problem of inflation (revealed most starkly once the exchange rate constraint had been removed) was due to the attempt to keep unemployment below its equilibrium level. If the government wanted to control inflation and achieve lower unemployment it had to use supply-side measures. A combination of demand-management and incomes policies would fail. Hence the quest, during the last 15 or more years, for effective supply-side policies. That task has been made more difficult by the apparent rise in the equilibrium rate of unemployment over the post-war period.

After that rapid tour we can take a slightly more leisured look at post-war events.

The thread on which I hang this story is successive Budgets. It will be obvious from the foregoing that this is not as satisfactory for the later period as it is for the earlier period, As Lord Lawson says in reference to his 1984 Mais Lecture: 'It follows from the thesis set out in the Mais Lecture that the promotion of jobs and employment is not the Treasury's principal responsibility' (Lawson, 1992, p. 423). However, Budget speeches do provide convenient statements about how the government sees the economic challenges that face it and how it intends to meet them. Also supply-side measures that involve revenue or expenditure changes are typically announced in Budget speeches, with the 1994 one as a prime example.

My story begins with a White Paper rather than a Budget speech.

THE 1944 WHITE PAPER

The 1944 White Paper on employment policy is the obvious place to start an account of post-war policy. In its opening words it provides both a commitment and a theory of how that commitment can be met:

> The Government accept as one of their primary aims and responsibilities the maintenance of a high and stable level of employment after the War.
> A country will not suffer from mass unemployment as long as the total demand for its goods and services is maintained at a high level.

The White Paper is in effect an account of how aggregate demand affects employment and a guide to the ways in which aggregate demand could be regulated. It presented the theory in a simple and straightforward way. For example:

> Assuming a given level of wages and prices, and full mobility of labour, workers will lose or fail to find employment because there is not a sufficiently large expenditure on the goods and services which they might produce. If more money is spent on goods and services, then more money will be paid out as wages and more people will be employed.

Chapter IV of the White Paper included an elementary account of the multiplier and stressed the need to intervene at the first sign of recession. It made the following commitment: 'The Government are prepared to accept in future the responsibility for taking action at the earliest possible stage to arrest a threatened slump'.

It rejected the idea that recessions were self-correcting. It also suggested that fluctuations in expenditure on private investment and net trade were the main cause of the cycle. The guiding principles of government policy in maintaining total expenditure would be:

- the encouragement of higher exports;
- action to limit swings in private investment;
- public investment to be timed to offset swings in private investment;
- action to check and reverse cyclically-induced falls in consumption.

Chapter V of the White Paper explained how the government intended to maintain total expenditure, particularly on capital. For the moment, monetary policy was ruled out as an instrument because the government intended to follow a cheap money policy after the war. It might be reinstated later but even then it was not expected to be very effective:

> Monetary policy alone, however, will not be sufficient to defeat the inherent instability of capital expenditure. High interest rates are more effective in preventing excessive investment in periods of prosperity than are low interest rates in encouraging investment in periods of depression.

The government proposed to encourage firms to vary their capital spending counter-cyclically. It also planned to increase the flexibility of public capital expenditure. It recognized that the public would start by resisting the idea that public expenditure should be increased 'when incomes were falling and the outlook was dark' but believed that resistance could be overcome if people realized that periods of recession provided an opportunity to improve the 'permanent equipment of society'.

If, despite the government's efforts, there were cyclical swings in capital spending, the government would try to regulate consumption:

> Here again, speed will be essential. The ideal to be aimed at is some corrective influence which would come into play automatically – on the analogy of a thermostatic control – in accordance with rules determined in advance and well understood by the public.

The chosen method was a variation in social insurance contributions. The fund would move in and out of balance over the cycle. This system was not expected to come into effect for a few years. The government also said it would consider raising general taxation so that it achieved a budget surplus during the boom.

The White Paper's commitment to full employment was not unconditional and it required the cooperation of the public:

> the success of the policy outlined in this Paper will ultimately depend on the understanding and support of the community as a whole – and especially on the efforts of employers and workers in industry; for without a rising standard of industrial efficiency we cannot achieve a high level of employment combined with a rising standard of living.

In particular, the policy relied on low or zero inflation:

> Action taken by the Government to maintain expenditure will be fruitless unless wages and prices are kept reasonably stable. This is of vital importance to any employment policy, and must be clearly understood by all sections of the public. If we are to operate with success a policy for maintaining a high and more stable level of employment, it will be essential that employers and workers should exercise moderation in wage matters so that increased expenditure provided at the outset of a depression may go to increase the volume of employment.

(It may be noted, in passing, that the objection was not simply to inflation as such. The risk was that inflation would frustrate the attempts to expand real expenditure and employment.)

The success of the policy required that wages and prices be kept under control:

> Thus the stability of these two elements is a condition vital to the success of employment policy; and that condition can be realised only by the joint efforts of the Government, employers and organised labour.

It also required efforts from the workers:

> It would be a disaster if the intention of the Government to maintain total expenditure were interpreted as exonerating the citizen from the duty of fending for himself and resulted in a weakening of personal enterprise. For if an expansion of total expenditure were applied to cure unemployment of a type due, not to the absence of jobs, but to the failure of workers to move to places and occupations where they were needed, the policy of the Government would be frustrated and a dangerous rise in prices might follow.

(One can recognize here a precursor of the debate, which did not emerge fully until 1968, about the natural rate of unemployment.)

As we know, the White Paper was a compromise between the radicalism of the members of the economic section of the Cabinet (with Meade as principal author) and the conservatism of the Treasury which did not believe that demand-management would work and was extremely reluctant to accept Budget deficits.

FULL EMPLOYMENT IN A FREE SOCIETY

William Beveridge's book *Full Employment in a Free Society* (1944) is sometimes treated as if it had the same status as the 'Report on Social Insurance and Allied Services' (Beveridge, 1942) and represented official policy. But the 'Report on Social Insurance' was prepared at the government's request, with Beveridge as chairman of an inter-departmental committee, on which all the other representatives were civil servants. *Full Employment in a Free Society*, as Beveridge pointed out, was written by him as a private citizen 'with only such resources as could be made available to a private citizen during the war'. However, since the ideas influencing Beveridge were so similar to those that influenced the White Paper it is possible to think of Beveridge's book as a more full-blooded version of the White Paper, taking Keynesian ideas to extremes that would not necessarily have been accepted by Keynes himself.

Beveridge sent his manuscript to the printers eight days before the White Paper appeared. But 'the slow processes of private publication in war' allowed him to add a postscript before his book was published. Before we turn to that we consider the contents of the Report itself.

Beveridge saw the need to achieve full employment as a moral as much as a technical issue:

> Idleness is not the same as want; it is a positive separate evil from which men do not escape by having an income. (Beveridge, 1944, p. 18)

> The achieving of full employment would, without any other change, add largely to our material wealth. But that is the least of the changes it would make. It would add far more to happiness than to wealth, and would add most of all to national unity, by removing the misery that generates hate. (Ibid., p. 129)

Beveridge defined full employment as a state in which a seller's market for labour would be established by ensuring that the number of vacancies would exceed the level of unemployment. He believed that it would be possible to keep unemployment below 3 per cent.

The method for achieving full employment was in principle the same as that propounded in the White Paper:

> The first condition of full employment is that total outlay should always be high enough to set up a demand for products of industry which cannot be satisfied without using the whole man-power of the country: only so can the number of vacant jobs be always as high as or higher than the number of men looking for jobs. (Ibid., p. 29)

It was the state's responsibility to ensure that these conditions were met and the Budget would be the main method by which it did so:

> The Minister introducing the Budget, after estimating how much private citizens may be expected to spend on consumption and on investment together under a condition of full employment, must propose public outlay sufficient, with the estimated private outlay, to bring about that condition, that is to say to employ the whole man-power of the country. (Ibid., p. 31)

Beveridge proposed that aggregate demand could be kept to an adequate level by some combination of public expenditure increases and tax reductions (or by increases in public expenditure financed by tax increases).

Since Beveridge's commitment to continuous full employment was far more explicit than was implied by the White Paper, he paid greater attention to the dangers that such a commitment might produce particularly for the preservation of price stability. Under full employment with a seller's market for labour 'there is a real danger that sectional wage bargaining pursued without regard to its effects upon prices, may lead to a vicious spiral of inflation, with money wages chasing prices and without any gain in real wages for the working class as a whole'.

Beveridge was optimistic that the problem could be avoided. On the pay side he would rely on the unions:

> Organised Labour in Britain has sufficiently demonstrated its sense of citizenship and responsibility to justify the expectation that it will evolve, in its own manner, the machinery by which a better coordinated wage policy can be carried through. (Ibid., p. 200)

In return, the government would provide a price policy which would guarantee 'a stable value of money in terms of necessaries, with wages rising both in money terms and in real terms as productivity per head increases'.

In his postscript, Beveridge welcomed the White Paper. First, because it showed that the government at last intended to employ economists permanently. Second, because it rejected Treasury dogma as it had, for example, been propounded by Winston Churchill in his 1929 Budget speech:

> it is the orthodox Treasury dogma steadfastly held that, whatever might be the political and social advantages, very little additional employment and no permanent additional employment can, in fact, and as a general rule, be created by State borrowing and State expenditure.

Third, because the government accepted responsibility for maintaining high and stable employment.

He criticized the White Paper because it did not provide adequate means for controlling aggregate demand. He dismissed its proposals for influencing private investment, and he was sceptical about its proposals for public investment:

> The policy of the White Paper is a public works policy, not a policy of full employment. It amounts to little more than always having ready a five-year plan of public works of the established kind to be put in hand by the existing authorities, not when those works are most needed, but when private enterprise is slack. (ibid., p. 262)

Nor was Beveridge convinced by the proposal to vary demand by varying social insurance contributions. He regarded the practical and psychological difficulties of the proposals as considerable. More important, the proposal marked a significant difference between Beveridge and the White Paper. Beveridge's proposals were designed to achieve continuous steady expansion rather than to mitigate fluctuations.

In general he criticized the White Paper as far too cautious in relation to deficit financing. He referred to the much-quoted sentence in the White

Paper, 'None of the main proposals contained in this Paper involves deliberate planning for a deficit in the National Budget in years of sub-normal trade
activity' and commented, 'This is the old Treasury attitude, with self-decep-
tion added'. He concluded:

> The policy of the Government in future will be judged by its handling of eco-
> nomic, i.e. real, problems, not 'monetary' problems. Maintenance of the national
> income and maintenance of budgetary equilibrium are not 'equally' important.
> The former of them is fundamental – the first rule of national finance. The latter is
> subordinate, a local bye-law as compared with an Act of Parliament. (ibid., p. 265)

In terms of differences in diagnosis, Beveridge regarded as most important
the White Paper's emphasis on cyclical problems while he believed that there
was a problem of a chronic deficiency of demand. Beveridge's policy proposals were designed accordingly and among things he was prepared to accept
was continuous deficit spending. His final comments on the White Paper are
worth quoting at some length:

> Within the limits set by its social philosophy, the White Paper is a sincere attempt
> to deal with the disease of unemployment. But its brief diagnosis, admirable up to
> a point, understates the seriousness of the disease, that is to say the extent of the
> past failure of the unplanned market economy. And its practical proposals are
> inadequate, not only through deficient diagnosis, but even more because action is
> inhibited by a sense of values that is wrong in two respects: of treating private
> enterprise as sacrosanct – a sovereign power independent of the State, and of
> treating maintenance of budgetary equilibrium as of equal importance with full
> employment. (Ibid., p. 274)

THE POST-WAR YEARS

So we start the post-war period with a strong and weak version of the Keynesian
approach to employment policy. The White Paper offered techniques for offset-
ting recessions; Beveridge proposed that fiscal policy should be driven primarily and continuously by the need to maintain aggregate demand at a level
which was adequate to ensure full employment. The White Paper did not
expect there to be a problem of general unemployment in the years after the
war. It would be a period of shortages with possible local problems during the
transition from wartime to peacetime production. It was likely to be some time
before the policy for averting mass unemployment would be needed.

Certainly, the early post-war Budgets were concerned almost entirely with
problems of shortage leading to the risk of inflation or balance of payments
problems. In his 1947 Budget, Hugh Dalton boasted of his success in maintaining adequate aggregate demand:

Today there is plenty of purchasing power. That has been our aim. We have sought to lubricate the economic system with a sufficiency of purchasing power, much more evenly spread than before the war. That has been our aim and we have achieved it.

The immediate danger was inflation, but Dalton would not hesitate to run a Budget deficit (above the line) if the danger was deflation. He provided a spirited attack on those who wanted to end the cheap money policy and to replace it by an attempt to avoid inflation through a deflation of demand:

Let me be clear. If we were to follow through this policy of deflation, preached by some who sit in office chairs in the city of London, we would bring back dear money; we would bring back depressed trade; we would bring back mass unemployment; and we would bring back a clamour for cuts in wages and social services and for indiscriminate short-sighted economy campaigns of every sort. In my view, this must be resisted. It is intellectually wrong and morally reprehensible. This faction of whom I speak would enthrone the usurer, trample the common man in the dust, and consolidate catastrophe in our national life.

Dalton resigned immediately after the 1947 Budget. His successor, Sir Stafford Cripps, sought to control inflation by voluntary restraint. The *Statement on Personal Incomes, Costs and Prices* (Prime Minister, 1948) said there was no justification for any general increase in individual money incomes. The challenge was to restrain demand and costs in order to earn enough from exports to pay for the imports 'without which we can neither live nor produce'. The challenge dominated successive Budgets. In the 1950 Budget, Sir Stafford Cripps reminded the public that the government's aim was to create a happy country in which there was equality of opportunity: 'It is basic to that kind of life that there should be full employment and full participation by the workers in the industrial life of the community'.

The Budget speech included an explanation of fiscal policy which was rather closer to Beveridge than to the employment White Paper:

It is our unquestionable duty to avoid the twin evils of inflation and deflation. This we can only do by maintaining a balance between the amount of goods and services which the nation seeks to buy and the amount which can be produced when the labour force is, as at present, fully employed. Excessive demand produces inflation and inadequate demand results in deflation. The fiscal policy of the Government is the most important single instrument for maintaining that balance.

Excessive spending rather than inadequate demand was the problem. Hugh Gaitskell was faced by even more severe problems associated with massive increases in defence expenditure and the fall in the terms of trade associated with the Korean War. He introduced one of the toughest Budgets of the post-war period in order to help the balance of payments. He did not believe that a recession could cure a cost inflation and he recognized the difficult balance he had to achieve: 'Too severe a budget will cause losses, unemployment and austerity at home, without any substantial benefit to our external position'.

The Labour governments of 1945–51 were able to achieve full employment without any need for the deliberate use of fiscal policy. As the White Paper had predicted, the problem was one of excess demand and labour shortage. They were ready to use demand-management if the need arose but recognized that full employment could only be associated with price stability if employees exercised restraint.

CONSERVATIVE POLICIES 1951–55

R.A. Butler started his chancellorship with a balance of payments crisis and had to introduce a tough Budget but was then able to embark on a period of generosity. Emergency measures were introduced in November 1951 and Bank rate was raised from $2^{1}/_{2}$ to 4 per cent. It is difficult now to recall that a balance of payments crisis could almost be seen as a matter of life and death. In his 1952 Budget, Butler described what would have happened if the reserves had run out:

> we here in this island would, before the end of the year, have found ourselves unable to secure either our daily bread or the raw materials upon which both employment and production depends. There would have been expanding areas of real want and of growing unemployment.

So a policy to save the reserves was at the same time a policy to save jobs.

It appeared that there could be two sources of a balance of payments problem. The first was excess domestic demand; the second was an autonomous loss of competitiveness. The former could be solved by a tightening of policy. The accompanying rise in unemployment was regrettable. In the latter case, policy tightening was unlikely to work. In either case, wage and price moderation would help matters.

In the following years, as the balance of payments problem eased, Mr Butler was able to cut taxes in his pursuit of 'expansion without inflation'. The Budget was the means by which economic success could be delivered. As he said in 1954:

> the man in the street knows that the real value of the Budget lies in its contribution to those things which are really important to him – full employment, stable prices, a steady growth of production.

THE ECONOMIC IMPLICATIONS OF FULL EMPLOYMENT

By 1956, when Harold Macmillan was Chancellor of the Exchequer, the years of expansion had brought problems of inflation and the balance of payments. The year 1955 had been 'a year of great prosperity for the mass of ordinary men and women in this country. Everyone had a job ...'. Unemployment had been at record low levels throughout the year. The question was how full employment could be maintained without risks.

In March 1956, the government published *The Economic Implications of Full Employment* (Prime Minister, 1956). It pointed out that, apart from a few weeks in 1947, unemployment had been below 3 per cent since the war. For most of the period it had been below 2 per cent and it was now about 1 per cent. But inflation was threatening this success in achieving full employment:

> In the increasingly competitive conditions which have developed in world markets in the last few years, continually rising costs and prices in this country must inevitably weaken the whole basis of our export trade; and if we do not export enough, we shall be unable either to support a steady expansion of production at home or to maintain full employment.

Although the loss of competitiveness (under a fixed exchange rate) was the most serious consequence of inflation, it also produced other harmful effects: 'Continually rising prices are an obvious evil' because of their effects on income and wealth. Inflation would also discourage savings and hence the scope for investment.

Government policy would be directed at achieving full employment: 'In order to maintain full employment the Government must ensure that the level of demand for goods and services is high and rises steadily as productive capacity grows'. But this commitment to full employment allowed employers to make large pay claims and allowed employers to grant them: 'If the prosperous economic conditions necessary to maintain full employment are exploited by trade unions and businesses, price stability and full employment became incompatible'.

That did not mean that the country could choose to have low unemployment if it was prepared to accept high inflation, since that would produce balance of payments problems and the loss of the ability to buy essential imports. At any rate there was no necessary conflict between full employment and price stability. The solution lay in self-restraint in making wage claims and in fixing profit margins and prices so that total money incomes rose no faster than output.

The 1956 White Paper provides a valuable guide to the views which were to continue to dominate policy-thinking for most of the next two decades. A commitment to full employment certainly produced the risk of inflation since the government would be bound to accommodate any pay settlements agreed by employers and employees. It left the rate of inflation completely undetermined. (In practice, the fixed exchange rate provided a constraint and converted a threatened runaway inflation into a balance of payment crisis.) The government recognized the dilemma but was reluctant to use higher unemployment as a means of cutting inflation. This was for two reasons. First it wanted to maintain full employment and second it did not believe that a policy of deflation would work. High unemployment was not expected to be effective in reducing pay increases. This suggests that it believed that a high level of employment did not *cause* inflation but *permitted* it. (In the terms of the time, there was a cost inflation which was then accommodated by government policy.) Since high inflation produced no overall benefits (although it had distributional effects) the solution was to persuade everyone to moderate their pay claims and price increases.

Governments were prepared, reluctantly, to use deflation to avert a balance of payments crisis. That was because they knew it would work by reducing the demand for imports. Also, balance of payments crises by their nature required a policy response whereas a modest acceleration of inflation did not.

CONSERVATIVE POLICIES 1956–64

Although Mr Macmillan did not believe that deflation would reduce inflation he was required by the conditions of the time to cut demand in his 1956 Budget. The result was a slowdown of economic growth. The problem of inflation was still apparent when Mr Thorneycroft introduced the 1957 Budget. But he believed that the solution lay in voluntary restraint and in recognizing that the people had to respond to the responsibilities as well as the benefits of high levels of unemployment:

> There are some who say that the answer lies in savage deflationary policies, resulting in high levels of unemployment. They say that we should depress demand to a point at which employers cannot afford to pay and workers are in no position to ask for higher wages. If this be the only way in which to contain the wage/price spiral, it is indeed a very sorry reflection upon our modern society.

By 1958 when Mr Heathcoat-Amory was chancellor the economy was still experiencing the delayed effects of the earlier deflation. Unemployment was rising. In his Budget speech he said: 'Although we are still fully employed by any normal standard, there is rather more unemployment than a year ago – 2 per cent compared with 1.7 per cent in March last year'. But since price stability had not been fully obtained, it was too soon to contemplate any general relaxation of economic policy. The main need was to avoid the conditions which had caused a series of foreign exchange crises:

> In any case I am convinced that in present circumstances it is not a question of getting price stability at the cost of mass unemployment ... The real risk of large scale unemployment would arise if our currency lost its value or we lost our competitive power to such an extent that we could no longer afford to pay for our food and raw materials.

GDP fell in 1958. It produced for the first time a deliberate fiscal reflation in the 1959 Budget in order to reduce unemployment. (Monetary policy had also been eased, with Bank rate reduced steadily from 7 to 4 per cent.) Unemployment had reached 2.8 per cent in January 1959 and was falling but more needed to be done:

> Although the current level of unemployment is low in comparison with most other industrial countries, it is still too high. It must be our unceasing endeavour to get every person we can into productive employment without putting at risk the stability of the foundation of our economy on which the prospects for full and steady employment must rest.

Mr Heathcoat-Amory added: 'There is no greater waste than the human waste and misery of unnecessary unemployment'.

Since price stability had been achieved, a fiscal stimulus could be safely afforded. By 1960 there was evidence that the economy was recovering. Unemployment had fallen from 621 000 to 413 000 and employment had risen by 300 000. The recovery had however brought back balance of payments problems which persisted into 1961. Mr Selwyn Lloyd in his 1961 Budget claimed that inflation had been killed in 1958 and showed no signs of returning. However, poor supply-side conditions meant that the economy was very prone to balance of payments problems at only moderate rates of growth. In July 1961 a crisis produced a package of deflationary measures including a pay pause for the public sector. That in turn produced the quest for a more general incomes policy. The crisis also produced the National Economic Development Council (NEDC) and the National Economic Development Office (NEDO) as an attempt to relieve the supply-side problems to which Selwyn Lloyd had drawn attention.

NEDO announced that the economy was capable of annual growth of 4 per cent over the period 1961 to 1966. The Budgets of 1963 and 1964, with Mr Maudling as chancellor, were designed to bring growth up to that pace.

LABOUR POLICIES 1964-70

Mr Maudling's dash for growth did not succeed as he had hoped in removing the balance of payments constraint. The problem dominated policy-making by the Labour government that came to power in 1964. It was a matter first of attempting to avoid devaluation and then of responding to it once it had occurred.

All the Budgets concentrated on the balance of payments as the central policy problem. In 1965 Mr Callaghan said that the aim of the Budget was to produce a surplus on the combined current and capital accounts. In 1966 he reported that the government's mandate was to achieve three objectives at the same time – a strong pound, a steadily growing industrial strength and full employment. Since there were at present jobs for all, policy had to be directed to the balance of payments. And so the story continued. Policies to restore the balance of payments were backed up by attempts to control prices and costs through incomes policies. The 1967 devaluation produced, in Mr Jenkins's words, 'a stiff Budget, followed by two years of hard slog'. There was also the failed attempt to improve industrial relations in the Industrial Relations Bill 1969.

By 1970 Mr Jenkins judged that his policies had successfully shifted resources into the trade balance and felt able to provide a moderate stimulus to demand. But unemployment continued to rise.

CONSERVATIVE POLICIES 1970-74

By the time of Mr Barber's Budget in 1971 both inflation and unemployment were rising: 'Two problems, above all, command attention at the present time, inflation and unemployment: a new and, in many ways, a baffling combination of evils'. He believed that the rise in money wages had partly caused the rise in unemployment and he called for 'a progressive and substantial de-escalation of pay settlements'. Despite the rise in inflation he did not believe that demand should be reduced: 'I do not believe that the fight against inflation would be aided at present by any further lowering of the pressure of demand'.

Since the fight against inflation required greater confidence in the future progress of the economy he decided to stimulate the economy. The process was taken some way further in the 1972 Budget which was perhaps the second post-war Budget which was directed mainly at reducing unemployment: 'There is universal agreement that the present high level of unemployment is on every ground – economic and social – one which no government could tolerate'.

Mr Barber certainly did not believe that the high unemployment could be accepted as a means of defeating inflation: 'While cost inflation is clearly one of the causes of high unemployment, I have never agreed with those who look to unemployment as the cure for inflation'. Nor did he believe that faster growth would produce higher inflation:

> I do not believe that a stimulus to demand of the order I propose will be inimical to the fight against inflation. On the contrary, the business community has repeatedly said that the increase in productivity and profitability resulting from a faster growth of output is one of the most effective means of restraining price increases.

The stimulus of the 1972 Budget helped bring unemployment down by over 200 000 in a year. Its delayed effects, combined with the world boom, helped to produce a growth of GDP of over 7 per cent in 1973 and a further fall in unemployment. Mr Barber's optimism on inflation was not however justified and 1972 saw the introduction of a series of incomes policies which eventually had to cope with the consequences of the quadrupling of oil prices in 1973/74.

LABOUR POLICIES 1974–79

Mr Healey had to deal with the consequences of the oil price increase and the inflation associated with it. But he too was not prepared to deflate demand to cut inflation: 'I totally reject the philosophy that would cure the high blood pressure in the economy by bleeding it to death'.

In his second Budget, in November 1974, he reported that unemployment was rising less rapidly than expected. He hoped that the doubling of the regional employment premium he had announced in July might be one reason. He suggested that unemployment was more likely to rise than fall but he did not expect it to rise too high. But he warned that if wages rose beyond the limits set by the TUC the government would be forced to take steps to reduce demand, which would cause higher unemployment.

He also referred to the problem of the unequal pressure of demand for labour which could cause shortages for some skills in conditions of general unemployment: 'We need to develop a labour market policy such as has operated so successfully for many years in Sweden, based on an expansion of our provision for industrial training'. The general Budget stance was to ensure that the overall level of demand would be sufficient to prevent any danger of mass unemployment in the coming year.

By the Budget of 1975, inflation had risen to 20 per cent and unemployment was 3.2 per cent. Mr Healey said he had been pressed to take measures to cut unemployment but he was unable to do so because of the size of the balance of payments deficit, which was 5 per cent of GDP and because of the risk of higher inflation. He had to take steps to reduce the PSBR but found room to provide more money for the Manpower Services Commission and introduced the Temporary Employment Subsidy. He admitted that unemployment was likely to continue to rise and could reach 4 per cent (about 1 million) by the end of the year: 'The effect of the Budget measures on employment has given me great concern, since I absolutely reject the use of mass unemployment as an instrument of policy'.

The 1976 Budget was, above all, 'a Budget about jobs and about inflation, which is the main threat to jobs in Britain today'. He set a target of reducing unemployment to 3 per cent in 1979. He estimated that that would require annual growth of 5^1/$_2$ per cent a year in 1977, 1978 and 1979 and an annual increase in manufacturing output of 8^1/$_2$ per cent. He believed this was not impossible. The main risks were a temporary shortage of capacity and a balance of payments problem. He hoped that the industrial strategy and incomes policy would help reduce both risks.

In September 1976 the prime minister, Mr Callaghan, gave a speech to the Labour Party Conference which contains one of the best-known passages from any party leader's speech. I shall refrain from repeating it here but it is important to remember that a great deal of the speech was devoted to a discussion of unemployment and possible measures to reduce it. Unemployment (on today's definition) was 4.2 per cent. This was a rate which, in Mr Callaghan's words, 'cannot be justified on any grounds, least of all the human dignity of those involved'. But 'the cosy world we were told would go on for ever, where full employment would be guaranteed by a stroke of the Chancellor's pen, cutting taxes, deficit spending, that cosy world is gone'.

Since the Labour government rejected unemployment as an economic instrument, it had to understand the cause of high unemployment: 'Quite simply and unequivocally, it is caused by paying ourselves more than the value of what we produce'. Necessary parts of a policy to reduce unemployment included the social contract to moderate pay claims, the industrial strategy to improve the performance of the manufacturing sector and adequate profits to finance investment:

> Whatever we do in the short term, the only long-term cure for unemployment is to create a healthy manufacturing industry that will hold its own overseas, and in doing so it will then certainly be able to retain its grip on the domestic market.

Mr Callaghan listed the microeconomic measures that had been introduced to help reduce unemployment including the Job Creation programme, the Temporary Employment Subsidy, the Work Experience programme, the Youth Employment Subsidy and the Job Release scheme.

Mr Callaghan's speech is usually regarded as the turning point in the post-war history of employment policy. The words were clearly very important. They emphasized, but not for the first time, that the sustainable level of unemployment must depend on the relationship between wages and productivity. It followed that demand-management could not *on its own* be used to drive unemployment to some arbitrary level. Mr Callaghan was not, however, suggesting that unemployment could or should be used to control inflation. Nor was he denying that demand-management could be used, at least temporarily, to cut unemployment.

Mr Healey's Budget of 1977 did not suggest that there had been a revolutionary change. He said: 'The plain fact is that the present level [of unemployment] is unacceptably high; and action is clearly needed to improve the future prospect'. Mr Healey introduced a reflationary budget, although part of the reflation was conditional on success in keeping inflation under control. In his 1978 Budget he said that the transformation in the nation's financial status (following the IMF loan of 1976) had not yet been reflected in an adequate growth of output: 'In consequence unemployment remains intolerably high, though it has been falling since September'.

It was the first purpose of his Budget to encourage a level of economic activity sufficient to get unemployment moving significantly down. He said: 'Our main objective in the coming years, like that of other countries, must be to reduce the intolerable level of unemployment by stimulating demand in ways which create jobs at home without refuelling inflation'. He introduced an expansionary Budget but he warned that it would only be successful if inflation could be brought under control.

It may be sensible to take stock at this stage of the story. The brief survey at the beginning of the chapter mentioned the general tendency in the 1960s and 1970s to move away from market solutions. This tendency was associated with the attempt to establish a more corporatist state on the German or Scandinavian model. This was apparent, for example, in Mr Heath's attempts to achieve tripartite agreement on output, pay and profits. Under the Labour administrations of 1974 to 1979 it was embodied in the Social Contract.

A possible basis for this move was as follows. 'Keynesian' ideas suggested that the government could control real output through its control of aggregate demand and, therefore, the level of unemployment. Inflation was believed to be primarily in the hands of the employers and the unions, although the government could intervene directly through the use of prices and incomes policies. Since the government wanted low inflation it could offer low unemployment in exchange for it. It added further inducements (particularly to 'insiders') in the form of industrial policy directed at maintaining existing industry and special employment measures, such as the Temporary Employment Subsidy directed at maintaining existing jobs. Inducements to the unions for their co-operation included revisions to trade union law. The 'outsiders' were helped by measures such as the Job Creation programme etc. and by increasingly generous social security payments.

It is difficult to explain why this rejection of markets occurred. The spirit of the age, particularly in the 1960s, was notably anti-commercial but it is not clear whether that was cause or effect. This chapter has already referred to the puzzling combination of rising unemployment and rising inflation in the early 1970s which may have reinforced the idea that normal market constraints were breaking down, at least in the labour market. Mr Callaghan's 1976 speech offered an alternative explanation for rising unemployment but did not appear to alter the thrust of policy. In retrospect it has been suggested that the accompanying microeconomic policies were raising the level of unemployment at which inflation would start to accelerate. They were therefore reducing the effectiveness of demand-management policy. They were also raising the cost of cutting inflation.

THE ROAD TO 1979

We do not unfortunately have the equivalent of the employment White Paper to establish the agenda for the Thatcher and Major eras. There have been a large number of expositions of the Conservative government's approach to employment policies but most have appeared since around 1983.

Some rather general ideas about the conduct of economic policy under a Conservative government were set out in *The Right Approach to the Economy* in 1977. It was intended as a Shadow Cabinet paper but in the event was published in the names of its authors – Geoffrey Howe, James Prior, Keith Joseph and David Howell. The broad framework for policy was to be responsible free collective bargaining within a counter-inflationary policy based on control of the money supply. Responsibility was to be assisted by an economic forum 'where the major participants in the economy can sit down calmly together to consider the implications – for prosperity as well as for unemployment and pay-bargaining – of the Government's fiscal and monetary policies'.

The Right Approach stated: 'No sensible person can really imagine that we do not understand – and care about – unemployment'. There were no specific promises about the level of unemployment that would be achieved and no single solution to the problem. The conditions for higher employment included lower taxes and market-based pay bargaining. The latter required more responsible behaviour by the unions but it was hoped that this could be achieved voluntarily:

We see the trade unions as a very important economic interest group whose cooperation and understanding we must work constantly to win and to keep, as we have done in the past. We see no need for confrontation and have no wish for it. (Maude, 1977, p. 19)

(It has been suggested that this conciliatory approach explains why the report was not published as a Shadow Cabinet paper.) The authors did seek changes in the rules related to closed shops but hoped that they could be achieved through a voluntary code of conduct.

A more detailed account of thought on employment was provided by Sir Keith Joseph in *Conditions for Fuller Employment*, a lecture given to the Bow Group in 1978 and subsequently published by the Centre for Policy Studies. The lecture started, 'I seek common ground today in pursuit of a common objective: a substantial and lasting improvement in the bleak prospects for employment'. His solution was to rely on the free operation of the labour market with minimal interference from the government:

The market economy with safety nets has a stronger propensity towards full employment at high and rising living standards than an economy where government decisions constantly replace market decisions.

... a labour market, given favourable conditions – including an adequate, but not excessive growth in money supply – inclines naturally towards equilibrium between the supply of and the demand for labour, via the balancing factor of flexible wage rates, while maximising choice for employer and employee. The process *tends* – though there will always be some rigidities and distortions to mar the ideal – to provide as many jobs as there are people wanting jobs. (Joseph, 1978, p. 8)

Policies to favour employment therefore required policies to make the labour market operate more effectively. The impediments that Joseph identified included high government spending and borrowing; high taxation; price, pay and dividend controls; untaxed social security benefits; over-regulation; Luddism; union obstruction of pay flexibility; an inflexible council housing system; and the destruction of the rented housing market. Jobs were created by customers not by governments. They resulted from the attempts of 'myriads of individuals, entrepreneurs, managers, workers each striving to serve his own and his family's interests'.

It is for the state to create a framework – of lower taxes, stiff competition, adequate but not excessive regulation and a healthier relationship than now between net earnings and the net benefits of the safety net – to harness that self-interest to the national interest. (Ibid., p. 18)

Thus Keith Joseph was setting out much of the agenda that has been followed since 1979. The emphasis was to be on the supply side rather than on demand-management. The speech ended with a clear rejection of the commitment that had dominated so much of post-war economic policy: 'Full employment is not in the gift of governments. It should not be promised and it cannot be provided'.

Despite that comment, the lecture's title and its content suggested that Conservative policies would provide lower unemployment in due course than was being experienced at the time he spoke (about 4.3 per cent on current definitions).

Sir Keith Joseph had listed a number of supply-side failings. It is difficult to deduce the priorities between them but for some of the Conservative Shadow Cabinet, the role of the trade unions was paramount. For example, Lady Thatcher wrote in her (subsequent) memoirs:

> Unlike some of my colleagues, I never ceased to believe that, other things being equal, the level of unemployment was related to the extent of trade union power. The unions had priced many of their members out of jobs by demanding excessive wages for insufficient output, so making British goods uncompetitive. (Thatcher, 1993, p. 272)

Similarly, Lord Tebbit recalls part of his candidacy speech:

> the real causes of unemployment – the world recession and the uncompetitiveness of British industry which had been brought about by earlier Socialist policies and the activities of trade unions in wrecking businesses through excessive pay claims, constant strikes and a refusal to modernise working practices. (Tebbit, 1988, p. 191)

Lord Lawson has written: 'When we first took office in 1979, at the heart of the problem of Britain's malfunctioning labour market – and of a number of other ills besides – clearly lay the much-discussed trade union question' (Lawson, 1992, p. 436).

An important source for this emphasis on the role of unions was provided by Hayek. For example: 'There is no substitute for a flexible wage structure. The vain search for a palliative while preserving the unions' strengths is the chief source of Britain's economic decline' (Hayek, 1980, p. 21).

Hayek argued that the combination of trade union power and the government's commitment to full employment meant that it could not control inflation. He speculated on the means of producing low inflation and favoured a short, sharp shock:

> Even 20 per cent unemployment would probably be borne for six months if there existed confidence that it would be over at the end of such a period. But I doubt whether any government could persist for two or three years in a policy that meant 10 per cent unemployment for most of that period. (Hayek, 1980, p. 23)

The Conservative manifesto for the 1979 election listed five tasks as the first essential steps in rebuilding the economy and reuniting a divided and disillusioned people. The first two were:

1. to restore the health of our economic and social life, by controlling inflation and striking a fair balance between the rights and duties of the trade union movement;
2. to restore incentives so that hard work pays, success is rewarded and genuine new jobs are created in an expanding economy.

In relation to trade unions it proposed changes, which it would introduce at once, to the laws on picketing, on the closed shop, and on the use of secret ballots. It proposed lower taxes to encourage economic growth. On policies for jobs it said:

> Too much emphasis has been placed on attempts to preserve existing jobs. We need to concentrate more on the creation of conditions in which new, more modern, more secure, better paid jobs come into existence. This is the best way of helping the unemployed and those threatened with the loss of their jobs in the future.

CONSERVATIVE POLICIES 1979–84

Changes in the fiscal stance have not, since 1979, been used as an instrument for regulating unemployment. Thus Budget speeches are less important as a source of accounts of policy changes. However, Budget speeches have continued to be used as a means of describing the government's general approach to policy-making.

Sir Geoffrey Howe set out the new approach in the 1979 Budget. He argued that it was common ground that 'the poor performance of the British economy in recent years has not been due to a shortage of demand. We are suffering from a growing series of failures on the supply side of the economy'. He rejected the claim that his Budget was 'peversely contractionary' since that would imply that an alternative fiscal policy could produce more growth and more employment. An easing of fiscal policy could only serve to fuel the fire of inflation. He admitted that there might be a decline in activity; but that was inevitable while inflation was being brought under control. He warned against the consequences of trying to get higher pay increases to offset the indirect tax increases: 'Any attempt to have it both ways will simply end up by threatening jobs and putting firms – on which jobs depend – out of business'.

By 1981 unemployment had risen to about 8 per cent. In that year's Budget speech Sir Geoffrey Howe commented on the role of excessive pay claims:

> Many factories had already gone a long way towards pricing themselves out of the market by earlier pay settlements. Many of those who secured big pay increases may have improved their own standard of living, but only at the cost of pushing their fellow workers out of a job.

But matters were beginning to improve: 'Pay bargainers have begun to face up to the harsh truth that excessive pay is a major cause of unemployment'. He hoped that the government's policies would produce lower inflation and, in due course, lower unemployment.

The 1981 Budget was directed primarily to reducing the PSBR and bringing the medium-term financial strategy back on course. In 1982 it was possible to change the focus: 'This will be a Budget for industry – and so a Budget for jobs'. The speech included a long section on unemployment and its causes. Sir Geoffrey Howe quoted two figures that, he said, virtually told it all. Since 1960 the real purchasing power of the average citizen had risen by over two-thirds, but the real rate of return on the capital employed by British industry had fallen by five-sixths. 'In other words, our present living standards have for years been plumbed from the store of investment for the future.' Reflation of demand was not the solution to the problem of unemployment. The challenge was to help create the conditions in which the unemployed could obtain work in jobs that would last. He argued that the main problem was that wages were not flexible downwards.

In his 1983 Budget Sir Geoffrey Howe announced the Job Release scheme and the Enterprise Allowance scheme. He reported that special employment and training schemes were already helping 750 000 people.

In his first Budget, in 1984, Mr Lawson announced that he would continue the policies designed to defeat inflation. 'To abandon them would be to risk renewed inflation and much high unemployment.' But the faster inflation came down, the faster output and employment were likely to recover.

THE 1984 MAIS LECTURE

Mr Lawson's Mais Lecture, 'The British Experiment', was delivered in June 1984, at a time when inflation had been brought below 5 per cent but when unemployment was still rising (although employment had started to rise in 1983). He confronted the question of whether, having succeeded in bringing down inflation, the government should now turn its attention to unemployment. His answer consisted of an account of policy-making since 1979 and its rationale. He remarked:

Every Government is concerned about inflation, just as every Government is concerned about prosperity and unemployment. The question is, what is the cause of inflation and its cure, and what is the cause of unemployment and *its* cure.

He pointed out that for much of the post-war period the conventional wisdom had been that unemployment could be reduced by macroeconomic policy while inflation was increasingly seen as a matter to be dealt with by microeconomic policy – 'the panoply of controls and subsidies associated with the era of incomes policy'. But this assignment had been precisely wrong:

> It is the conquest of inflation, and not the pursuit of growth and employment, which is or should be the objective of macro-economic policy. And it is the creation of conditions conducive to growth and employment, and not the suppression of price rises, which is or should be the objective of micro-economic policy.

Microeconomic policy was being designed to make the economy work better and thus generate more jobs. The experience of the United States showed that 'the spirit of enterprise, and workers who prefer to price themselves into jobs rather than out of them, are a powerful engine of employment'. On the prospect for jobs Mr Lawson said:

> It is the rediscovery of the enterprise culture, operating within the framework of markets progressively liberated from rigidities and distortions, that will provide the only answer to the curse of unemployment and the only true generator of new jobs.

CONSERVATIVE BUDGETS 1985–93

In his 1985 Budget, Mr Lawson repeated the themes he had discussed in his Mais Lecture. The government's strategy had two key components – monetary policy to reduce inflation and supply-side policy to improve the competitive performance of the economy:

> The supply side is rooted in profound conviction born of practical experience both at home and overseas, that the way to improve economic performance and create more jobs is to encourage enterprise, efficiency and flexibility; to promote competition, deregulation and free markets; to press ahead with privatisation and to improve incentives.

He said that his overriding objective in the Budget was to improve the prospect for jobs:

Jobs are created by firms that are competitive, efficient, profitable and well managed. That in turn requires a workforce with the right skills, one that is adaptable, reliable, motivated and prepared to work at wages that employers can afford to pay.

The government's role was limited. It could not legislate for the spirit of enterprise or prevent Luddism. It could not stop unions pricing themselves out of work. It could however remove obstacles to the effective working of the labour market, correct deficiencies of education and training and provide a good system of taxation: 'Our attack on the evil of unemployment is clear, coherent and strong'. Mr Lawson announced that he would expand the Youth Training scheme, change unfair dismissal legislation and seek to reform the Wage Councils. While the emphasis was on the supply-side measures, macroeconomic policy would ensure adequate monetary demand: 'the medium-term financial strategy is as firm a guarantee against inadequate money demand as it is against excessive money demand'.

Mr Lawson returned to the question of unemployment in his 1986 Budget. The solution to the problem required progress on two key fronts – sustained improvement in the performance of business and industry and a level of pay which enabled workers to be priced into jobs instead of pricing them out of jobs. It was on the latter front that the UK failure lay: 'The plain fact is that labour costs per unit of output in British business and industry continue to rise faster than is consistent with low unemployment ....'

The problem lay not just in the level of pay but also in the rigidity of the pay system. If all the adjustment during a recession were made to quantities rather than prices then redundancies were inevitably more likely to occur. A possible way out was to link pay to profitability per head. He announced that he intended to discuss profit-related pay with employers. Meanwhile he would continue to support the Youth Training scheme and the Community programme. He also announced some new active employment measures, including Job Start, Restart and Job Club. The Enterprise Allowance scheme was to be expanded and a New Workers scheme for 18–20 year olds was to be introduced.

In his 1987 Budget Mr Lawson, following the Green Paper, introduced a scheme to encourage profit-related pay: 'Profit-related pay is no panacea. But then there are no panaceas.' In the 1988 Budget which included the cuts in the standard and higher rates of income tax, Mr Lawson said that the outlook for exports and jobs would depend critically on employers keeping their costs firmly under control: 'The tax relief that I introduced last year for profit-related pay will, in time, help to increase pay flexibility and to improve the working of the labour market'. But he wanted to make it easier for people to move to where new jobs were. Hence his extension of the Business Expansion scheme to include residential lettings, with the aim of encouraging the expansion of the private rental market.

By 1989 Mr Lawson was having to restrain demand in order to avoid inflation: 'The task of business and industry is to control their pay and other costs. The more successfully they do so, the less costly in terms of output and employment the necessary adjustment will be.' As a supply-side measure Mr Lawson announced a reform of national insurance contributions to remove a serious work disincentive from the system.

There was no mention of unemployment in Mr Major's only Budget, in 1990. By 1991 Mr Lamont returned to the topic. He emphasized the importance of the supply side. It was still necessary to provide a more flexible labour market and a better-skilled labour force: 'If wages are inflexible, the burden of recession falls disproportionately on jobs; it is the only way for employers to cut costs'. Mr Lamont said he would encourage profit-related pay and provide further support for employee share-option schemes. He would also provide additional tax relief for training. In his 1992 Budget Mr Lamont said he would continue with supply-side reforms. He also warned that a sustained reduction in unemployment over the longer term would depend crucially on success in keeping inflation down.

In his 1993 Budget Mr Lamont pointed out that unemployment in Europe was much higher than anywhere else in the world. It could not be reduced simply by stimulating demand. The solution was more flexible markets for goods and labour. The government would assist by helping the unemployed to rejoin the labour force and would resist 'job-destroying measures emanating from Brussels'. New measures included the Business Start-up scheme, an education allowance for the long-term unemployed, the Community Action scheme and an experimental Benefit Transfer scheme.

SUPPLY-SIDE POLICIES SINCE 1979

The foregoing account of Budgets since 1979 has included references to the supply side both as a general area of policy concern and as the rationale for the introduction of specific measures. However, since supply-side policies have, as Mr Lawson pointed out in his Mais Lecture, been the main method of encouraging higher employment they need to be discussed in greater detail. Unlike the general stance of fiscal policy they have not, in the main, been the primary responsibility of the Treasury.

I have mentioned that before 1979 the Conservative party had already switched its attention to supply-side policies as a means of tackling the problem of unemployment. There was no commitment to full employment but it was argued that labour market reform, deregulation, and cuts in taxation and public expenditure would provide favourable conditions for higher employment. It was recognized that the defeat of inflation would raise unemployment temporarily but there was no published estimate of what the increase would be nor any promises about what level of unemployment would be achieved in the longer term. Given the emphasis on the role of the trade unions, particularly by Mrs Thatcher, the first steps were taken in this direction. The Employment Acts of 1980 and 1982 made secondary picketing illegal, tightened the conditions for closed shops and made trade unions liable, through their funds, for any unlawful acts which they or their senior officials committed. These measures on trade union reform were accompanied by the promised cuts in income tax and measures to deregulate markets. There was also a series of special employment measures.

In 1985, against a background of further rises in unemployment, the government published a White Paper, *Employment: The Challenge for the Nation* (Cmnd 9474), to describe its general approach to the problem and to explain the policies it had introduced. It provides a useful summary of the approach to employment policy during the first five or six years of the Conservative administration. Its first task was to promote nationwide understanding of the origin and nature of unemployment which, it said, posed the sharpest challenge to whole country. In a phrase reminiscent of Sir Keith Joseph's Bow Group lecture it said 'Jobs come from customers and from nowhere else'. The challenge was to understand why that process did not seem to work effectively in the UK and to see what could be done to improve it.

The government's strategy for guiding and supporting the national effort for jobs had three interlocking parts:

- a sound and stable framework of economic and industrial policy, with the defeat of inflation as the first priority;
- particular forms of encouragement of jobs, including the removal of obstacles which discourage employers from taking on workers and the introduction of schemes to improve the quality of the work force;
- direct action to tackle severe and deep-seated problems of unemployment for groups particularly hit by changes in industry.

The White Paper stated that the biggest single cause of the UK's high unemployment was the failure of the labour market – the weak link in the economy. The labour market needed to be improved in a number of ways:

- in quality, so that businesses can find the increasingly demanding skills they need, now and in the future;

- in cost and incentives, so that people are neither prevented from pricing themselves into jobs nor deterred from taking them up;
- in flexibility, so that employers and employees adapt quickly to new circumstances;
- in freedom, so that employers are not so burdened by regulation that they are reluctant to offer more jobs.

The Paper showed what steps had been taken and would be taken to provide these improvements. Steps to improve the quality of the labour force included:

- proposals on education, including the development of the curriculum and changes to the 16-plus examinations;
- the Technical and Vocational Education Initiative;
- the Youth Training scheme, which provided work-based training for school-leavers, was to be extended to provide job-related training for all 16–18 year olds.

Labour market flexibility was to be assisted by

- schemes such as Job Release which enabled older men and women to retire early provided their job was taken by an unemployed person;
- improvements in industrial relations;
- measures to reduce the labour costs borne by employers (e.g. by abolishing the national insurance surcharge) and to increase the incentives to move out of unemployment and into work (e.g. by changes in income tax thresholds and national insurance contributions);
- reform of Wage Councils;
- changes in employment protection law.

The White Paper also listed the measures that had been taken to help the unemployed directly, including the Enterprise Allowance scheme, which paid the unemployed £40 a week while they started their own businesses and the Community programme which provided work in the local communities for the long-term unemployed. It argued that such measures were far more cost-effective than money spent on extra public investment or subsidies to industry. On their own the special measures described in the White Paper could not cure unemployment but 'these carefully targeted and cost-effective measures will help many of those worst hit by unemployment and will improve their chances of getting back into work.'

In its discussion of labour market flexibility the White Paper raised the question of the level of real wages:

The higher the real cost of labour the lower employment will be, both because employers will be forced to economise on labour, and because higher labour costs mean lower profits and competitiveness, less investment and less business.

A more rapid growth of productivity would be a welcome solution to the problem but what was needed was a slower growth of earnings. The White Paper pointed out that despite recession and higher unemployment, those in work continued to enjoy steady increases in real earnings. The Treasury had published a study earlier that year (HM Treasury, 1985) showing that employment could increase considerably if people accepted slightly lower earnings growth. The answer did not lie in incomes policies:

> Experience of pay policies shows the Government cannot sensibly intervene directly. Employers and workers must strike their own bargains for their own circumstances. But they should recognise the consequences for their own and their customers' competitiveness, and for expectations elsewhere. The biggest sufferers from excessive wage rises are the unemployed. There is little evidence despite expressions of concern that employers and unions negotiating for those in work have yet appreciated the effect of wage increases on the chances the unemployed have of finding jobs.

The White Paper could not offer a simple solution to this problem, although it hoped that its measures to reduce employment costs and to increase the incentives to take up work would help.

One may perhaps detect some sense of disappointment in the White Paper that the achievement of low inflation and the measures of union reform and deregulation had not yet produced lower unemployment. As Lord Lawson commented, 'As the 1980s wore on I became more and more convinced that employers rather than unions were responsible for pay settlements incompatible with high employment' (Lawson, 1992, p. 432). Lord Lawson's support for profit-related pay was based on this recognition of an insider–outsider problem. (The proposal was partly stimulated by his reading of Weitzman's *The Share Economy* (Weitzman, 1984).)

In recent years the government has taken further opportunities to describe its policies towards employment. We can start with *What Does Full Employment Mean in a Modern Economy?* which was a memorandum submitted to the House of Commons Employment Committee by the Department for Employment in November 1993. It includes an account of policy since the war and comments on the shortcomings of the approach during the 1960s and 1970s:

- increased labour market regulation;
- schemes to 'save' jobs which were more likely to reduce efficiency than to affect output or employment;

- reduced incentives to work because of the increased generosity of unemployment benefits;
- bad industrial relations supported by legislation favouring the unions;
- failure to invest adequately in training and education.

These developments made the UK particularly ill-suited to respond to the supply shocks of the 1970s and early 1980s.

The memorandum implicitly criticizes some of the policies of the early 1980s, particularly those that attempted to reduce unemployment through special schemes that encouraged individuals to withdraw from the labour market:

> There may be social reasons for such a policy but its economic effects tend to be damaging. Such a policy, by reducing labour supply may reduce unemployment in the short term but damage the economy and employment in the longer term since it reduces the economy's ability to produce goods and services (the economy's productive potential).

During the 1980s there had been a general shift, in terms of employment policies, towards encouraging and helping the unemployed to compete effectively for the available jobs. Policies which attempted to reduce unemployment by encouraging employers to retain their existing work forces had been phased out in the early part of the decade.

Also during the 1980s the employment measures had increasingly focused on ensuring that the unemployed retained work skills and confidence. Hence the training programmes and the formation of the Training and Enterprise Councils (TECs) at the end of the 1980s. The latter helped to tailor training to the needs of local labour markets. This shift of focus also included the introduction of Restart and a stricter benefit regime. The emphasis was on 'active labour market policies' rather than on the passive payment of benefits.

The memorandum argues that the concept of 'full employment' was not useful as a guide to policy: 'the Government's aim is to reduce the level of unemployment consistent with low and stable inflation'.

The memorandum repeats the general lines of the government's approach and describes some new labour market measures, including:

- Training for Work, as a scheme to help the long-term unemployed find work and acquire skills;
- Youth Credits, to allow young people to have a greater choice of training;
- Investors in People, to encourage employers to increase the skills of their employees;
- further development of NVQs;
- The Career Development loan to help people pay for their own vocational training.

It also listed the schemes designed to bring the unemployed into active participation in the labour market and into competition with existing workers. These schemes had been made more effective by integrating unemployment benefit offices and jobcentres. They included:

- Restart interviews;
- Job Clubs;
- Work Trials;
- The Job Interview Guarantee;
- Job Plan workshops.

The government also set out its views in *Competitiveness and Employment* which it submitted to the G7 Jobs Conference, following the Tokyo Summit of July 1993 and in the chapter on Employment in the *Competitiveness White Paper*. In each case it emphasized the need for structural policies if unemployment was to be permanently reduced.

The competitiveness White Paper listed the requirements on people who receive unemployment and related benefits:

- to be available for work;
- to seek work actively;
- to seek work widely and to be prepared to accept any job after a period of more restricted job search;
- to attend six-monthly interviews to review their job search activity and receive offers of help;
- to respond positively where directed towards suitable employment opportunities;
- to attend a Job Plan workshop or Restart course when they pass the 12- or 24-month thresholds of unemployment and turn down all other offers of help.

The government had made beneficiaries aware that failure to comply with these requirements could result in loss or reduction of benefits.

The White Paper described a number of new initiatives, particularly the government's programme of active market measures, including new Restart courses, the Workwise course and 1-2-1 Interviews for 18–24 year olds. It also described the jobseeker's allowance which will be introduced in 1996 to replace income support for unemployed people and unemployment benefit: 'It will emphasise the responsibilities of unemployed people who are paid unemployment benefits, whilst at the same time offering improved help to get back to work as quickly as possible.'

Competitiveness and Employment describes fully the philosophy and actions which have comprised the government's policy on employment during the past 15 years. It provides a summary of the measures to help the unemployed to compete effectively (see Appendix A to this chapter).

MR CLARKE'S MAIS LECTURE 1994

Mr Clarke's Mais Lecture 'The Changing World of Work in the 1990s' was presented almost precisely 50 years after the employment White Paper. He stated that unemployment would remain the main preoccupation of policy-makers in the 1990s but argued that no serious policy-maker thought that the problem was solely one of inadequate demand.

He described the UK approach as emphasizing the efficient functioning of the labour market. He pointed out that the labour market in the USA was more flexible than that in Europe but he believed that its social consequences for the unemployed and the low paid were unacceptable. He said:

> I have always proclaimed my belief that our objective should be to combine the best aspects of the two approaches: American enterprise and free market efficiency with the European commitment to the welfare state. I have never believed that the two are incompatible.

He rejected the idea that international competition or technological change had caused structural unemployment to rise. He suggested four ways in which the government could help reduce structural unemployment:

- ensuring a flexible labour market;
- helping individuals to adapt through active labour market measures and training;
- helping those who are out of work by providing an adequate social safety net;
- continually seeking to improve incentives to participate in the labour market.

He described the measures the government had already introduced and in particular stressed the role of small businesses in creating jobs. He also defended the growth of part-time work as evidence of a flexible labour market. He accepted that the pace of change created fears and uncertainties among men and women in every walk of life. He denied that making industry and markets more efficient could only come at the expense of social justice: 'I believe that a strong welfare state can complement, not hinder, more flexible markets by reducing fear of change and opposition to it.' He also said it was important that the social security system should complement an efficient labour market. He referred to the changes in national insurance contributions he had made in his November Budget and said that the government was looking at the extent to which the welfare system distorted incentives at the lower end of the income scale.

He closed with a reference to the 1944 White Paper:

> I am as committed as the author of that paper to a 'high and stable level of employment': we shall get there not by pursuing simply a flexible labour market or simply a strong welfare system, but by recognising that the two must reinforce each other. Both are essential in the world of work in the 1990s.

THE 1994 BUDGET

Neatness would suggest that we end the story in May 1994 with the Chancellor of the Exchequer's Mais Lecture 'The Changing World of Work in the 1990s' almost precisely 50 years after the publication of the employment White Paper. I shall sacrifice neatness for completeness and end with the Budget of November 1994 which incorporated some of the proposals in the Mais Lecture.

Mr Clarke said that one of the priorities of his Budget was to create more jobs, particularly for people who had been out of work for some time. Unemployment remained far too high. The labour market and trade union reforms of the 1990s had helped unemployment to start falling at a much earlier stage of the recovery than previously. It would continue to fall:

> But, I have long believed, as my Panel of Independent Forecasters points out and as is now widely recognised, that demand expansion on its own is not enough to produce a sufficient fall in unemployment. We have to do more to reduce unemployment in ways which are consistent with sustained growth and low inflation.

His new measures were designed to help unemployed people back to work and reduce the cost to employers of recruiting unemployed people. The measures were particularly targeted towards the long-term unemployed. They included: changes in Training for Work, extension of measures to keep the unemployed in touch with the labour market (the 1-2-1 and Workwise schemes) and extension of the Community Action programme. The measures to encourage employers to recruit unemployed people, particularly the long-term unemployed, included: a reduction in employer national insurance contributions for the lower paid, a national insurance holiday (from 1996) for employers who take on the long-term unemployed, an expanded Work Trials scheme and new Workstart pilot schemes.

The Budget also included measures to ease the transition from unemployment to work, including: speeding up the payment of benefits for those who take jobs, the extension of the job-finder's grant and a tax-free back to work bonus. In addition there were measures to help people who wanted full-time work and a pilot scheme for providing in-work benefits for people without children.

Mr Clarke said: 'The days of priming the pump to cut unemployment are long since past'. The aim, continuing the tradition of the previous 15 years, was to introduce policies to cut structural unemployment.

THEORY AND ACTIONS – A POSTSCRIPT

This is not an attempt to present a complete account of the development of economic thought about unemployment since the war. Nor is it a critique of policy actions in the light of such theoretical developments. Rather, as I said at the start of the chapter, it is an attempt to relate policy to the academic developments that accompanied or, more usually, preceded them.

Much of the discussion has to be speculative; there is very rarely any direct evidence about academic sources but we can see government policy responding to a combination of economic events and external ideas.

One way of describing the changes in the approach to employment policy during the period is to say that the government was seeking the answer to the following questions: What is the nature of equilibrium in the labour market? How is it defined and how is it determined? One can add another closely related question: What is the cause of inflation?

I suggest that the current stance of policy is consistent with the following answers to the questions:

- equilibrium in the labour market is the point at which the supply of and demand for labour are equal;[1]
- supply and demand depend on structural conditions (e.g. taxes, social security arrangements, technology, etc.);
- they may also depend on the past history of unemployment;
- the steady state of inflation is set by monetary conditions;
- disequilibrium in the labour market causes inflation to decelerate or accelerate.

Those answers suggest that the way to reduce unemployment (except possibly in the very short term) is to alter the conditions which affect the supply of and demand for labour.

At the beginning of the story, a possible answer to the question about labour market equilibrium would have been the following: equilibrium in the labour market is achieved at the level of employment at which aggregate demand equals output. That is recognizable as the first-year undergraduate version (vintage *c*. 1959) of 'Keynesian' economics. Of course we would now recognize that it is not the whole story and it must, at any rate, be part of the current version of equilibrium in the labour market. So it is a question of emphasis. The early version emphasized aggregate demand, the current version emphasizes aggregate supply. Our task is to trace the evolution of policies and thought that led governments to shift from one version to the other.

If we take the 'Keynesian' version (I do not need to explain why the inverted commas are necessary) as a sufficient answer to the question and if the government can control aggregate demand, then the government can control the level of employment. It follows that the labour market will be in equilibrium at any level of output. An alternative way of expressing the same idea is that aggregate supply is infinitely elastic over the relevant range. That may be contrasted with the implied current view that aggregate supply is inelastic (perhaps infinitely so).

Put in those terms, whatever the first-year textbooks may have implied, policy-makers have not usually behaved as if aggregate demand was all that mattered. Certainly the Employment White Paper and *Full Employment in a Free Society* (Beveridge, 1944) were both written by people who were aware that there were risks of inflation at high levels of employment. A more reasonable description of policy-makers' views (though not in terms they would use or recognize) was that aggregate supply was highly elastic up to a point and increasingly inelastic beyond it. That point could be defined as 'full employment'.

We can have little difficulty in identifying the source of the emphasis on aggregate demand in determining unemployment. Beveridge acknowledged his source: 'A new era of economic theorizing about employment and unemployment was inaugurated by the publication in 1936 of *The General Theory of Employment, Interest and Money* by J.M. Keynes, now Lord Keynes' (Beveridge, 1944, p. 93).

The White Paper was written by James Meade among others and was seen (and criticized) by Keynes. Despite the inconsistencies, which largely reflected the attempt to incorporate the Treasury orthodoxy on Budget deficits, the White Paper was an attempt to put Keynesian ideas into practice.

Why might a policy directed at high employment cause problems of inflation? I think we can distinguish two slightly different stories. In the first, inflation is endogenous and in the second, it is quasi-exogenous. The first was set out by Keynes in *How to Pay for the War* (1940). Excess monetary demand at full employment would cause prices to rise until incomes and output were equal. Such conditions were particularly likely in wartime and could continue in the post-war period – hence the need for deflationary budgets to close the 'inflation gap'. But it was also possible that a government, in its attempts to raise aggregate demand sufficiently to ensure full employment, would overdo it and cause inflation. If full employment was not a single point but a range over which shortages of goods or labour progressively appeared one could see why attempts to reduce unemployment increased the risk of inflation.

The quasi-exogenous story runs as follows. If economic agents know that the government is committed to full employment they know that it must accommodate any inflation rate they generate. Thus there is no constraint on pay or price increases and inflation becomes indeterminate. In practice, under a fixed exchange rate system, the process will be brought to an end by a balance of payments crisis. Both stories can be recognized in the post-war policy statements. The Employment White Paper, as already discussed, also warned that increases in prices could frustrate an attempt to achieve a high level of employment if additional money demand caused higher prices and wages rather than higher output and employment.

Those two versions of the inflationary process also provide two slightly different rationales for incomes policies as a means of combining low unemployment with low inflation. On the one hand, they can be seen (in modern terms) as a supply-side policy, designed in particular to shift the supply curve of labour. On the other, they can be seen as regulating nominal wages and avoiding a quite unnecessary process of inflation in which both employers and employees are prepared to accept the real wages associated with high employment.

As the narrative sections of this chapter have already shown, the early post-war years produced problems of excess rather than inadequate aggregate demand, and fiscal policy responded accordingly. But the accompanying risk of inflation was both undesirable in its own right and presented a threat to high employment because of its potential effect on the balance of payments. It was not surprising therefore that governments sought to relieve the inflationary constraint by trying to persuade employers and employees to co-operate with each other and with the government in controlling inflation, particularly if they believed that increases in unemployment would be ineffective.

In 1958, A.W. Phillips published 'The Relation Between Unemployment and the Rate of Change of Money Wage Rates in the United Kingdom, 1860–1957'. He suggested that the statistical evidence from the period he studied showed that the rate of change of money wages could be explained by the level of unemployment and the rate of change of unemployment (apart from years in which import prices rose rapidly). He also suggested that, on the basis of the historical relationship, stability of product prices could be achieved if unemployment were kept at a little under $2^1/2$ per cent.

This paper was, of course, immensely important in the development of academic thought on inflation. It confirmed the policy-makers' view that lower unemployment was associated with higher inflation. It also offered an explanation for the relationship. Phillips suggested that the relationship he had discussed was an example of the general response of prices of goods or services to the level of demand:

> When the demand for labour is high and there are very few unemployed we should expect employers to bid wage rates up quite rapidly, each firm and each industry being continually tempted to offer a little above the prevailing rates to attract the most suitable labour from other firms and industries. On the other hand it appears that workers are reluctant to offer their services at less than the prevailing rates when the demand for labour is low and unemployment is high so that wage rates fall only very slowly. The relation between unemployment and the rate of change of wage rates is therefore likely to be highly non-linear. (Phillips, 1958, p. 283)

That last sentence also seemed to justify another of the policy-makers' beliefs, namely that deliberate attempts to raise unemployment in order to reduce inflation were likely to be ineffective.

The Phillips curve seemed to offer a clear choice for the policy-makers. Textbooks could include a simple representation of the choice they faced, using a social welfare function and a representation of the inflation–unemployment trade-off, with the normal tangency conditions for the choice of the optimum. If the Phillips curve was a correct account of the constraints the policy-makers faced, it suggested that they could always achieve lower unemployment if they were prepared to accept higher inflation. Alternatively, it provided an incentive to shift the Phillips curve in a favourable direction by using incomes policies.

It is difficult to know whether the Phillips curve changed the conduct of policy or simply confirmed the beliefs that the policy-makers already held. From 1958 to 1971, policy-making can be described within a Phillips curve framework. Policy was expanded in response to rising unemployment. Incomes policies were used in an attempt to improve the trade-off between unemployment and inflation and/or the balance of payments. Despite incomes policies, balance of payments problems occurred at ever higher levels of unemployment. The devaluation of 1967 was an attempt to change the balance of payments constraint. By 1971 both unemployment and inflation were rising at the same time. This experience called in question the Phillips curve apparatus and new explanations were sought. They included socio-political explanations in terms, for example, of rising trade union militancy.

They also included explanations of why faster growth could be accompanied by lower inflation. Mr Barber's Budget of 1972 suggested that he accepted these explanations and believed that an expansion of demand could produce both lower unemployment and lower inflation.

In 1968 a paper was published which provided an alternative explanation for the events of 1971. Professor Milton Friedman's presidential address 'The Role of Monetary Policy' can reasonably be described as the most important contribution to the employment debate in the post-war period. Almost everything about unemployment or inflation that has been published since then can be seen as an attempt to develop the ideas that were presented in that paper. Most importantly for this review it provided a new answer (or revived an old answer) to the question about labour market equilibrium:

> At any moment of time, there is some level of unemployment which has the property that it is consistent with equilibrium in the structure of *real* wage rates .... 'The natural rate of unemployment', in other words, is the level that would be ground out by the Walrasian system of general equilibrium equations, provided there is embedded in them the actual structural characteristics of the labour and commodity markets, including market imperfections, stochastic variability in demands and supplies, the cost of gathering information about job vacancies and labour availabilities, the costs of mobility and so on. (Friedman, 1968, p. 8)

The phenomenon of simultaneous increases in unemployment and inflation could, in Friedman's framework, be explained by changed price expectations in response to the devaluation of 1967, so that the price expectations term (in an augmented Phillips curve) was dominating the unemployment term. Most importantly, Friedman suggested that, for a given set of structural conditions, the equilibrium level of unemployment was unique. Demand-management could, at best, be used to offset a temporary shift in aggregate demand. Unemployment could only be reduced permanently if structural conditions were changed. Friedman's ideas are implicitly recognized in Mr Callaghan's 1976 speech with its emphasis on real wage behaviour and its rejection of demand-management as a means of regulating unemployment. Policies consistent with Friedman's approach have been followed since 1979.

Friedman emphasized that the word 'natural' did not imply that the equilibrium level of unemployment was immutable and unchangeable: 'On the contrary, many of the market characteristics that determine its level are man-made and policy-made'. His paper in effect established the programme of research to discover what actually determines the equilibrium level of unemployment and what can be done (consistently with other policy objectives) to reduce it.

The influence of Friedman on UK policy was based not only on his analysis of the labour market but also on his studies of monetary policy. Since he and his followers seemed to be right about the consequences of the monetary expansion of the early 1970s they gained credibility for their views on the labour market, The shift of emphasis away from demand-management towards concern with the supply side can be associated with the following types of policy, which were introduced progressively from 1979 onwards:

- trade union reform;
- changes in the tax and social security system;
- deregulation in product and labour markets;
- abolition of Wage Councils;
- housing market reforms.

The immediate academic response to Friedman's paper was to investigate more deeply the nature of the expectations-augmented Phillips curve and to examine dynamic paths from one equilibrium to another. One line of research, led by Lucas (1972, 1973) produced the policy-ineffectiveness theories which implied that only unanticipated demand-management policies have real effects. That conclusion in turn suggested that the cost (in terms of higher unemployment) of cutting inflation might be small. Some of that optimism was shared by academic supporters of the post-1979 counter-inflationary policies. Another line of research produced the search theories as an explanation of the duration of unemployment and the willingness of the unemployed to adjust their wage aspirations (Phelps, 1970).

A further impulse to research was provided by the economic events of the 1970s with the combination, in much of the world, of rising unemployment and high inflation. This concentrated attention on the level of equilibrium unemployment rather than on the dynamics of disequilibrium. Bruno and Sachs (1985) particularly stressed the importance of the response of the labour market to the commodity price shocks of the 1970s and early 1980s and the central role of labour market conditions. Subsequent theoretical and empirical modelling of the equilibrium rate of unemployment then began to focus on the role of labour market imperfections and drew upon the twin 'efficiency wage' and union literatures. In these models the equilibrium wage is too high – and there is thus job rationing and unemployment – either because firms find it profitable to offer high wages in order to elicit greater effort from their employees, or because unions have sufficient bargaining power to raise wages above market-clearing levels. Contributions in this vein include Layard, Nickell and Jackman (1991) and Phelps *et al.* (1994). Deviations around this equilibrium unemployment rate are then as in Friedman–Lucas, but most of the interesting action is in the equilibrium rate itself.

However, the difficulty in finding empirically satisfactory explanations for the apparent increase in equilibrium unemployment in Europe also led researchers to suggest that the path of equilibrium unemployment might itself depend on past realizations of actual unemployment and thus be history-dependent ('hysteresis' theories). One strand of this literature emphasizes the fact that those responsible for setting wages do not care about the unemployed (an idea taken up in the 1985 White Paper) (Blanchard and Summers, 1986; Lindbeck and Snower, 1990). Another emphasizes the fact that the long-term unemployed are less attractive to employers and become demotivated (see Layard and Nickell, 1987; Budd, Levine and Smith, 1988).

It is not possible to establish direct links between any of this work and actual policy decisions but one could reasonably conclude that the academic research has provided a climate of opinion in which the government takes a fairly eclectic approach to supply-side measures. The Budget of 1994 is a case in point. The emphasis on measures to keep the unemployed in touch with the labour market can be linked to the problem of hysteresis. The schemes to reduce the cost of employing the low paid (by subsidies to the employer or by in-work benefits to the employer) can also be related to hysteresis and to insider–outsider problems. The proposals to tighten the work test in the move to the jobseekers allowance can be associated with the work of Layard and Nickell.

The development of employment policies in recent years suggests that identification of high unemployment as primarily a supply-side rather than as a demand problem is the beginning rather than the end of the story.

APPENDIX A: MEASURES TO HELP UNEMPLOYED PEOPLE COMPETE EFFECTIVELY

from 'Competitiveness and Unemployment' *(HM Treasury and DE, 1993)*

The range of measures offered in the UK to help unemployed people find work includes the following.

Help with Job Search

Mainstream Placing Services

- Network of over 1200 Employment Service local offices
- Jobcentres giving unemployed people access to a wide range of local and national job vacancies
- Target of 1.47 million unemployed people placed into work in 1993/94

Job Clubs

- For those unemployed over six months
- Provide guidance and training on job search techniques
- Stationery, stamps and telephones are all provided
- Brings people together in a mutually supportive environment
- 295 000 opportunities at a cost of £54.6m in 1993/94

Job Interview Guarantee

- For those unemployed over six months
- Employer guarantees interviews in return for enhanced vacancy filling service
- Enhanced services include matching individual jobseekers to vacancies and providing job preparation courses
- 300 000 opportunities at a cost of £30m in 1993/94

Job Search seminar

- For those unemployed over 13 weeks
- Provides information on how best and where best to look for employment
- 75 000 opportunities at a cost of £4.8m in 1993/94

Job Review workshop

- For those unemployed over 13 weeks
- Helps people to review their career progress and the options open to them
- Intended particularly for unemployed people with experience of professional and executive employment
- 40 000 opportunities at a cost of £3.5m in 1993/94

Advice and Motivation

Restart interview

- Mandatory for all those reaching six months' unemployment, repeated every six months
- Advice given to assist long-term unemployed people to take up opportunities (work, training, etc.)

- Enables public employment service to confirm clients are available for and actively seeking work
- Over 3 million interviews conducted in 1993/94

Job Plan workshop

- Mandatory week-long course for those unemployed for 12 months who refuse other offers of help
- Offers one-to-one assessment and guidance to help clients develop an effective plan to get back to work
- 300 000 opportunities at a cost of £37m in 1993/94

Restart course

- Week-long mandatory programme for those unemployed for 24 months who refuse other offers of help
- Helps long-term unemployed people reassess their strengths and skills, rebuild their motivation and self-confidence
- Helps clients consider other options in detail and decide what action to take to get back to work
- 110 000 opportunities at a cost of £11.5m in 1993/94

Work Experience

Work trials

- For those unemployed over six months
- Enables employers to assess the suitability of long-term unemployed clients for a vacancy before committing themselves to employing them
- Enables unemployed people to prove themselves in a real job while their benefits continue to be paid to them
- Trial period lasts for up to three weeks

Community action

- For those unemployed for over 12 months
- Provides a stepping-stone back into employment
- Offers part-time work of benefit to the local community and structured help with job search
- Mainly delivered by voluntary and charitable organizations
- 60 000 opportunities at a cost of £31.5m in 1993/94

Training

Training for work

- For those unemployed for over six months
- Provides appropriate training and structured work activity in line with individually assessed needs
- Aims to help people find jobs and improve their work-related skills
- 320 000 opportunities at a cost of £790m in 1993/94.

NOTE

1. The use of the expression 'labour supply' is intended to include the idea of the wage-setting schedule. I am not implying that policy-makers assume that there is a market-clearing equilibrium without job-rationing.

REFERENCES

Addison, P. (1975), *The Road to 1945*, London: Jonathan Cape.

Beveridge, W.H. (1942), *Social Insurance and Allied Services*, Cmnd 6404, London: HMSO.

Beveridge, W.H. (1944), *Full Employment in a Free Society*, London: Allen & Unwin.

Blackaby, F.T. (ed.) (1978), *British Economic Policy 1960–74*, Cambridge: Cambridge University Press.

Blanchard, O.J. and Summers, L. (1986)1 'Hysteresis and the European Unemployment Problem', *NBER Macroeconomics Annual*, 15–78.

Britton, A. (1994), 'Full Employment in a Market Economy', TUC/EPI Conference Paper.

Broadberry, S.N. (1991), 'Unemployment' in N.F.R. Crafts and N. Woodward (eds), *The British Economy Since 1945*, Oxford: Clarendon Press.

Bruno, M. and Sachs, J. (1985), *Economics of Worldwide Stagflation*, Cambridge, Mass: Harvard University Press.

Budd, A.P., Levine, P. and Smith, P. (1988), 'Unemployment, Vacancies and the Long-Term Unemployed', *The Economic Journal*, **98**, 1071–1109.

Cairncross, A. (ed.) (1989), *The Robert Hall Diaries 1947–1953*, London: Unwin Hyman.

Cairncross, A. (ed.) (1991), *The Robert Hall Diaries 1954–1961*, London: Unwin Hyman.

Clarke, K. (1994), 'The Changing World of Work in the 1990s', *Mais Lecture*, City University Business School.

Conservative Central Office (1979), *Conservative Manifesto 1979*.

Department for Social Services (1985), *Reform of Social Security: Programme for Action*, Cmnd 9691, London: HMSO.

Department of Employment (1985), *Employment: The Challenge for the Nation*, Cmnd 9474, London: HMSO.

Department of Employment (1993), *What Does Full Employment Mean in a Modern Economy?*, memorandum to the Employment Select Committee, House of Lords Library.

Department of Trade and Industry, HM Treasury and others (1993), *Competitiveness: Helping Business to Win*, Cmnd 2563, London: HMSO.

Friedman, M. (1968), 'The Role of Monetary Policy', *American Economic Review*, **58** (1), 1–17.

Hayek, F.A. (1980), *1980s Unemployment and the Unions*, Hobart Paper 87, London: Institute of Economic Affairs.

HM Treasury (1985), *The Relationship Between Employment and Wages*.

HM Treasury and Department of Employment (1993), *Growth, Competitiveness and Employment in the European Community*.

Institute of Economic Affairs (1978), *Trade Unions: Public Goods or Public 'Bads'?*, London: IEA Readings 17.

Johnson, C. (1991), *The Grand Experiment: Mrs Thatcher's Economy and How it Spread*, Harmondsworth: Penguin Books.

Jones, R. (1987), *Wages and Employment Policy 1936–1985*, London: Allen & Unwin.

Joseph, Sir K. (1978), *Conditions for Fuller Employment*, London: Centre for Policy Studies.

Keynes, J.M. (1936), *The General Theory of Employment, Interest and Money*, London: Macmillan.

Keynes, J.M. (1940), *How to Pay for the War*, London: Macmillan.

Lawson, N. (1984), 'The British Experiment', *The Fifth Mais Lecture*, City University Business School.

Lawson, N. (1992), *The View from No. 11*, London: Bantam Press.

Layard, R. and Nickell S.J. (1987), 'The Labour Market' in R. Dornbusch and R. Layard (eds), *The Performance of the British Economy*, Oxford: Clarendon Press.

Layard, R., Nickell, S.J. and Jackman, R.A. (1991), *Unemployment: Macroeconomic Performance and the Labour Market*, Oxford: Oxford University Press.

Lindbeck, A. and Snower, D. (1990), *The Insider–Outsider Theory of Unemployment*, Cambridge, Mass: MIT Press.

Lucas, R.E. (1972), 'Rational Expectations and the Neutrality of Money', *Journal of Economic Theory*, **4**, 103–24.

Lucas, R.E. (1973), 'Some International Evidence on the Output–Inflation Trade-Off', *American Economic Review*, **53** (3), 326–34.

Maude, A. (ed.) (1977), *The Right Approach to the Economy*, Conservative Central Office.

Ministry of Reconstruction (1944), *Employment Policy*, Cmnd 6527, London: HMSO.

National Economic Development Council (1963), *Conditions Favourable to Faster Growth*, London: HMSO.

Peden, G.C. (1988), *Keynes, the Treasury and British Economic Policy*, London: Macmillan.

Phelps, E.S. (1970), *Macroeconomic Foundations of Employment and Inflation Theory*, New York: Norton.

Phelps, E.S., Hoon, H.T., Kanaginis, G. and Zoega, G. (1994), *Structural Slumps: The Modern Equilibrium Theory of Unemployment, Interest and Assets*, Cambridge, Mass: Harvard University Press.

Phillips, A.W. (1958), 'The Relation Between Unemployment and the Rate of Change of Money Wage Rates in the United Kingdom, 1860–1957', *Economica*, **25** (100), 283–99.

Prime Minister (1948), *Statement on Personal Incomes, Costs and Prices*, Cmnd 7321, London: HMSO.

Prime Minister (1956), *The Economic Implications of Full Employment*, Cmnd 9725, London: HMSO.

Prior, J. (1986), *A Balance of Power*, London: Hamish Hamilton. ·

Tebbit, N. (1988), *Upwardly Mobile*, London: Weidenfeld and Nicolson.

Thatcher, M. (1993), *The Downing Street Years*, London: Harper Collins.

Tomlinson, J. (1985), *British Macroeconomic Policy Since 1940*, London: Croom Helm.

Weitzman, M.L. (1984), *The Share Economy: Conquering Stagflation*, Cambridge, Mass.: Harvard University Press.

Winch, D. (1969), *Economics and Policy*, London: Hodder and Stoughton.

6. Unemployment and the economists: a concluding comment

Walter Eltis

Three themes pervade this book. The first is the contrast between the significance of unemployment in the lives of between one-tenth and one-third of British families in the 19th and 20th centuries and the absence until Keynes of serious attempts by economists to produce a comprehensive theory of its explanation. Bernard Corry and Jose Harris have much to say about this, while Terry Peach offers a forerunner of 20th-century debates in the contrasting contributions of Thomas Malthus and David Ricardo to the explanation of the severe unemployment which followed the Napoleonic Wars.

A second theme is the gradual emergence of Keynes's analysis, its initial triumph as it was successfully applied to policy throughout the English-speaking world and its subsequent ineffectiveness in these countries. Bernard Corry, George Peden and Alan Budd have much to say about the contributions of Keynes and Keynesian policy and of subsequent disappointments.

A third theme is the manner in which much of the most useful analysis of British unemployment came from civil servants. Because unemployment mattered greatly to families and to governments, the senior civil service analysed its causes and the practical feasibility of the advice which came from the economics profession which had neglected the subject until its importance became inescapable. Harris, Peden and Budd each have much to say about the contributions of the Civil Service to the analysis and amelioration of unemployment in Britain.

The contributions to analysis and policy of the civil service and the academic economics profession are becoming closer at many levels which is underlined in Budd's contribution to this volume. Since 1992 he has been Head of the Government Economic Service and the government's Chief Economic Adviser. Earlier in his career he was a leading participant (with Sir Terence Burns, his predecessor as Chief Economic Adviser) in the work of the London Business School which provided much of the academic foundation for the policy framework which guided economic policy in the 1980s and the 1990s. The late 19th-century schism which Harris documents between academic economists who ignored unemployment and a concerned civil service which sought to alleviate it is far in the past.

None the less while many academic economists and civil servants speak the same language and are equally concerned to reduce unemployment, the collapse of practical Keynesianism has produced a near policy vacuum which resembles the one in the early 20th century. Then as now there appeared to be an unacceptable unemployment level of about 8 to 10 per cent. Corry quotes Mark Casson to the effect that the policies which governments and most academic macroeconomists now emphasize are precisely those which were most favoured in the 1920s (see p. 24). So is there still a way forward?

Budd concludes his contribution with the comment that, 'The development of employment policies in recent years' are 'the beginning rather than the end of the story' (see p. 130). This chapter will conclude with an indication of a possible way forward which owes much to Keynes but which is more long term than the policies he envisaged. Before that, I shall comment on the central themes of the preceding chapters.

WHY ECONOMISTS IGNORED UNEMPLOYMENT UNTIL KEYNES

David Ricardo and Thomas Malthus founded the Political Economy Club in 1821 and in the next century its membership included all Oxford and Cambridge professors of political economy, prime ministers (Gladstone attended and spoke frequently), chancellors, senior civil servants, bankers and prominent financial writers and editors such as Walter Bagehot. Between 1821 and 1921 the Club met seven or eight times a year and discussed employment or unemployment just four times.[1]

On 25 June and 3 December 1821 Ricardo and Malthus successively put the questions, 'Whether Machinery has a tendency to diminish the demand for labour?' and 'On what does the demand for Labour depend?' After that there was silence about the demand for labour and unemployment until 1 March 1895 when Sir John Macdonnell, a senior civil servant put the question, 'What are the best means of dealing permanently with the question of the unemployed?' and ten years later on 1 March 1905 the Bishop of Stepney (later Archbishop of York) asked, 'How is the problem of the unemployed in London to be best met at the present time and in the future?'

The silence of the economists but not the civil servants and bishops on unemployment underlines Harris's marvellous contribution to this volume which follows her definitive book on unemployment in the late 19th century and her biography of William Beveridge. As she remarks here in Chapter 3, of the books and articles on unemployment which 'began to pour forth from the mid 1890s none was written by an "academic" professional economist. They came instead from amateurs; from journalists, practical reformers, heretics and cranks', (p. 52) among whom she includes the Beveridge of the first decade of the 20th century.

The first edition of Palgrave's *Dictionary of Political Economy* which was published in three volumes in 1894–1900 has no article on unemployment. It contains a one paragraph article on employment by Edwin Cannan which includes the sentence:

> In a great community where co-operation in the production of wealth is effected by means of exchange, the fact that there is always a certain small proportion of persons seeking employment who are unable to find it is chiefly due to the circumstance that, owing to the division of employments, every kind of production comes to be carried on by people who have by training and experience acquired particular skill in that kind of production, so that when the demand for any one commodity slackens and the number of those who produce it has to be reduced, or at any rate not increased at its normal rate, the persons deprived of this employment are not immediately absorbed into other employments. (Cannan, 1894, vol. 1, p. 707).

Cannan's article also contains the phrase that, 'in all countries the able-bodied unemployed, including not only the men "out of work", but all others who from whatever cause are not engaged in labour, are but a minute fraction of the whole able-bodied population'. And that is all that Palgrave's *Dictionary* had to say about unemployment in 1894 when it was 6.9 per cent of trade unionists and it had been more than 10 per cent a decade earlier in 1886 (and before that in 1879). *The New Palgrave Dictionary of Economics* published in 1987 (Eatwell *et al.*) has substantial articles on unemployment, natural rate of unemployment, employment, full employment, involuntary unemployment and structural unemployment.

The likeliest explanation of Cannan's apparent unawareness of the scale of unemployment in the 1880s and the 1890s and the neglect of unemployment by most of the economists who preceded him was the general assumption that in the absence of trade unions and institutional rigidities, the labour market would clear. With that assumption the effect of a reduction in the demand for labour is lower wages and not unemployment. The analysis of the great classical economists indicated that lower wages would produce increased mortality at the poorer end of the income scale, and if wages fell far enough, there would be extra deaths among the young, the old and indeed the able-bodied in many labouring families. The tendency of a fall in the demand for labour was therefore to produce an increase in deaths but not additional unemployment, and this was thoroughly discussed by many leading political economists. By the mid-19th century, the wages of the averagely skilled and even the unskilled had risen to a level where a reduction in the real pay of the employed would no longer produce a significant increase in mortality. Only the casually employed remained vulnerable, so there was no longer a powerful tendency for a reduction in the demand for labour to reduce the size of the potential labour force.

Once that classical mechanism had ceased to operate, the principal way in which a reduction in the demand for labour caused social damage became its tendency to produce growing unemployment. This had always been present, and in the chapter 'Paper Money, Employment and Wealth' in his magisterial *Before Adam Smith* (1988) Terence Hutchison sets out the full extent to which the 17th-century pamphlet literature and modern economic historians have found a clear tendency for reductions in demand to produce unemployment and not merely reduced real wages.

Institutional money wage rigidities pervade the literature which Hutchison describes and there are also rigidities in Peach's Chapter 2 in this book on the Malthus–Ricardo debate. These were significant to Malthus but not to Ricardo. But the essence of the Malthus-Ricardo controversy is not whether a reduction in effective demand will produce unemployment rather than deaths through famine. It focuses on whether aggregate effective demand exists in an economy independently of potential supply, and especially whether demand can fall short of potential supply. Peach argues convincingly that Malthus failed to produce an account of his theory of effective demand which was clear to his contemporaries, or indeed, that has been clear to anyone since.

Peach's contribution to the reinterpretation of Malthus's theory of effective demand so that it can be rigorously restated will arouse much interest. His interpretation of Malthus's strongest line of argument is that public expenditure on public works and other kinds of immediately unproductive activity will, with a balanced budget, reduce the capital stock in agriculture and industry: and with normal assumptions, a reduction in the capital stock will raise the equilibrium rate of return on capital. Ricardo's response, and he evidently understood Malthus to be saying exactly what Peach attributes to him, was devastating. In his manuscript notes on Malthus's *Principles of Political Economy* which he sent on to Malthus immediately after its publication in 1820, he wrote:

> A body of unproductive labourers are just as necessary and as useful with a view to future production as a fire, which should consume in the manufacturers warehouse the goods which those unproductive labourers would otherwise consume. (Ricardo, 1951, p. 421)

and

> How can they in their consumption give value to the results of the national industry? It might as justly be contended that an earth-quake which overthrows

my house and buries my property, gives value to the national industry. (Ibid., p. 436)

A fire or an earthquake would reduce the capital stock and this could be expected to raise the marginal rate of return on the capital that remains, but Ricardo ridicules any suggestion that this can be good political economy. Peach is merely saying that Ricardo did not believe that attempts to raise demand in the short-term would be helpful when he says that it was his recommendation that, 'the government should do precisely nothing against a background of collapsing markets and soaring unemployment. The problem was merely one of a momentary lapse of reason on the part of the capitalist class.' (p. 47). Ricardo acknowledged in a much quoted letter to Malthus of 24 January 1817 that:

you have always in your mind the immediate and temporary effects of particular changes – whereas I put these immediate and temporary effects quite aside, and fix my whole attention on the permanent state of things which will result from them. Perhaps you estimate these temporary effects too highly, whilst I am too much disposed to undervalue them. (Ricardo, 1952b, p. 120)

Peach acknowledges that Ricardo had policy proposals which could have a favourable long-term impact, 'he held steadfastly to the position that the only helpful policies would be the repayment of the national debt and, over the longer term, the deregulation of trade' (p. 30). On 16 May 1822, two years after his notes on Malthus, Ricardo told the House of Commons in one of his most prescient statements:

were the corn laws once got rid of ... this would be the cheapest country in the world; and ... we should find that capital would come hither from all corners of the civilized world. Indeed such a result must be certain if we could once reduce the national debt ... If this were done, and if the government would pursue a right course of policy as to the corn laws, England would be the cheapest country in which a man could live; and it would rise to a state of prosperity, in regard to population and riches, of which, perhaps, the imaginations of hon. gentlemen could form no conception. (Ricardo, 1952a, pp. 167–8).

The reasoning which lies behind this powerful statement is that reductions in tariffs and in the taxation required to pay debt interest (which dominated Britain's budget after 1815) would reduce the marginal costs of production of British farmers and manufacturers. This would increase the rates of profit they could earn in conditions of normal trade, and as a consequence the equilibrium rate of return on capital would rise throughout the economy. These higher profits would produce long-term capital accumulation (whatever happened in individual cycles) which would favourably influence the *long-term* demand for labour and the equilibrium size of the population.

It is arguable that this policy package which went on to become orthodox financial policy for all 19th-century British governments had the favourable long-term effects on Britain's capital stock and population which Ricardo predicted.

Ricardo's long-term policy prescriptions therefore had great force, but as Peach makes very clear, he had no coherent analysis of what would influence employment in the short-term. There is nothing unusual in the history of economics in a policy framework (and institutions to implement it) which seeks to get the long-term right in a manner which may preclude short-term fine tuning. The creation of a politically independent Bundesbank in Germany with no brief to fine-tune employment can be interpreted in precisely these terms, as can British budgets in the 1980s which were based on the implementation of a medium-term financial strategy which ignored the short-term, most notably in 1981 when Sir Geoffrey Howe raised taxation while unemployment was high and rising.

Harris remarks that from 1870 to 1914 there was 'no serious theoretical challenge' among 'university-based economists' to the relevance to employment policy of 'the master paradigm of Ricardo and Adam Smith' (p. 52). It was therefore widely recognized that Ricardo (together with Smith) had left a 'master paradigm' to later political economists. These included McCulloch who wrote most of the economic articles in *The Edinburgh Review* in the next three decades and John Stuart Mill whom everyone read, who reiterated the advantages of free trade and economies in public expenditure.

But the university-based economists who were guided by the Ricardian paradigm of what was required for long-term prosperity evidently failed to concern themselves with the microeconomic functioning of the labour market which the Civil Service, the Church and the socially concerned recognized as significant.

There have always been rigidities in the labour market, and with the growth of trade union membership, assisted by late-19th century and early-20th century legislation, the impact upon unemployment of such rigidities arguably grew. With these increased rigidities, unemployment became higher, and an economic model where the labour market cleared and the Civil Service was left to tidy up the debris ceased to satisfy the economics profession. Its reaction crystallized in the evolution of Keynesian macroeconomics which dates from well before 1936.

THE IMPACT OF KEYNES AND OF KEYNESIAN MACROECONOMICS

The patent failure of the labour market to clear in the 1920s when British unemployment exceeded 10 per cent in every single year severely embarrassed those who still saw unemployment as primarily frictional. As Corry strongly brings out in Chapter 1 of this volume, the key development which established the possibility of a Keynesian approach which was to dominate the next half century was an appreciation that there were circumstances where much unemployment could be involuntary. He says that involuntary unemployment only began to be referred to in the early twentieth century and he gives as its standard definition, 'those out of work who are actively seeking work at the current wage rate and are available immediately for work.' (p. 15). He goes on to quote Keynes's more precise definition from the *General Theory*:

> Men are involuntarily unemployed if, in the event of a small rise in the price of wage goods relatively to the money-wage, both the aggregate supply of labour willing to work for the current money-wage and the aggregate demand for it at that wage would be greater than the existing volume of employment. (Keynes, 1936, 1973, p. 15)

If on Corry's definition there are unemployed workers willing to take work at the existing real wage, and on Keynes's that these will even take work at a *lower* real wage, extra effective demand will raise employment without an inflationary increase in wages.

It was very clear in Britain in the 1920s that there was extensive involuntary unemployment on the Corry definition so the labour market could no longer be characterized as one where unemployment was merely the product of frictions and rigidities. There was therefore a need for a new theory which took the economic challenge of extensive involuntary unemployment into account, and Keynes supplied it.

The most direct way of bringing the involuntarily unemployed into employment was through extra public works and it was on these that Keynes who (with Hubert Henderson) was advising Lloyd George, focused.

Peden dates the impact of Keynes on the analysis of employment policy from Lloyd George's proposals for public works in the 1929 General Election campaign. Before public works could be implemented, the arguments of the senior civil servants in HM Treasury who advised the chancellor and held the 'Treasury view' that public works would fail to raise employment had to be overcome. The Treasury succeeded in persuading Winston Churchill who was chancellor in 1929 that Lloyd George's policies would not work, and Philip Snowden, his Labour successor, that they should not be attempted.

Peden provides an account in Chapter 4 of how the 'Treasury view' evolved and of Keynes's efforts to counter it. It is evident that the strongest line of argument which Keynes had to destroy from 1929 onwards rested on the Treasury's assumption of a given money supply which could not be added to through the creation of extra government credits to pay for public works without inflationary risks which were politically and economically unacceptable. If the assumption of an unchanged money supply is accepted, most economists would agree with the Treasury that additional public works would raise interest rates. In the *General Theory* of 1936 Keynes evolved the argument that a depressed economy would often have a 'liquidity trap' which contained idle 'speculative' money balances which could be absorbed at an unchanged rate of interest into the larger 'transactions' balances which would be needed as the public works programme succeeded in raising output and employment. In these circumstances extra public works would not necessarily raise interest rates and crowd-out private sector investment.

But in 1929–31 Keynes had not yet discovered the liquidity trap and he made much use of Richard Kahn's multiplier which was formally presented in print in 1931. If the level of output in the economy was below potential as a result of the existence of extensive involuntary unemployment, extra public works would raise the national income, and once this had risen, the finance for the higher level of investment would be provided from this higher national income without any need to crowd-out any existing private sector investment projects. Keynes implicitly argued in 1929–31 that if there was sufficient saving to finance higher investment, there would be no need for interest rates to rise.

After 1936 the theory of the multiplier was often presented as if the rise in national income which follows extra public works is instantaneous. In Peden's chapter, the scope which this kind of unrealistic assumption offered to Keynes's Treasury critics is mercilessly exposed. They pointed out that, 'the lag between income being earned and tax being paid was, on average, 20 months in the case of income tax, and 32 months in the case of surtax ... and during this period the budget would remain unbalanced'. The Treasury officials went on to say that, 'it is no good saying that the works will produce the savings for investment, for *ex hypothesi* the borrowing precedes the works'. Peden goes on to say that, 'Keynes had to admit that the Treasury was right, and that 'dishoarding' (i.e. the mobilization of idle savings) and credit expansion were a necessary preparation for the process, described in the *General Theory*, whereby increased investment was accompanied by increased saving' (pp. 83–4).

Keynes failed in his various debates with the Treasury in the 1930s because the Treasury model included a series of detailed assumptions which were more realistic than those in his highly theoretical book which incorporated the developing theoretical apparatus he was evolving. The *General*

Theory was addressed to the world's economists, but the liquidity trap and other highly simplified concepts such as the instantaneous multiplier will have bemused those in the City to whom Treasury officials turned when they sought practical advice about the likely impact of policies upon markets.

This meant that Keynes had virtually no impact on the policies successive chancellors pursued in the 1930s. Their actual policies of balanced budgets until the need for rearmament became overwhelming proved far more effective than those in the United States. There were no public works prior to rearmament apart from those which could be expected to earn a rate of return comparable with that in the private sector, but with continually balanced budgets, Bank rate was held at 2 per cent until World War II, and unemployment fell from 2 830 000 in 1932, to 1 480 000 in 1937. In these five years in which unemployment fell by 1 350 000, employment grew by 2 690 000 and entirely without Keynesian policies Britain achieved one of the strongest recoveries in the world.

Keynes's triumph was in the academic economics profession but the Treasury remained indifferent. Peden quotes Grigg, principal private secretary to several chancellors, to the effect that Keynes's successive proposals were no more than 'different manifestations of a thesis that nations, unlike private individuals, can live so as to both have their cake and eat it' (p. 78).[2]

After 1937 with rearmament and the pressures of war the 'Treasury view' was buried, the national debt escalated, and Keynes came to the Treasury and brought many academic economists with him. Unemployment fell to lower levels than had ever been recorded, and it remained below 2 per cent until the 1960s. During the war Keynes conquered the Treasury, he inspired budget speeches (and may even have written one of Anderson's) and national income accounting which was one of the many by-products of the new economics of the *General Theory* helped to form a basis for post-war budget judgements. Budd (Chapter 5) documents the powerful initial influence of Keynesian analysis on post-war economic policy.

In addition to the conquest of unemployment after the war, inflation was remarkably subdued. It rose to a peak of 10 per cent after the devaluation of sterling in 1949 but after that it gradually fell back to 1 per cent in 1959 when unemployment was still no more than 2 per cent. In 1959 Britain had a 'discomfort index' (the sum of unemployment and inflation) of no more than 3 per cent, perhaps an all-time record.

The triumph of the post-war Keynesian approach to policy was largely confined to the English-speaking world. He had far less impact in France and Germany. Herbert Giersch, the first chairman of Germany's Council of Economic Experts (the 'wise men'), has provided an account of how he found an Adam Smith in his British prisoner of war camp in 1945, which became 'crucial to my view of the world' (Giersch, 1986, p. 255) and he was unimpressed by British and American Keynesians who came to Germany to lecture. Joan Robinson came to Münster shortly after the war to, 'expound a vulgar Keynesianism ... it was like Hamlet without the Prince of Denmark: a theory and policy of full employment without wages', while American Keynesians who were visiting Germany recommended 'expansionist policies, erroneously assuming that we had Keynesian unemployment rather than the classical variety arising from the influx of refugees and the destruction of the capital stock' (Ibid., p. 257).

Ernst Helmstädter, a more recent member of the Council of Economic Experts, explains that by the time Giersch became chairman in 1963, he had developed a very unKeynesian view of the assignment problem. According to Helmstädter (1988, p. 414), Giersch had come to believe that inflation depended upon the growth of the money supply which was determined by the Bundesbank, while employment depended upon 'the level and structure of real wages' and fiscal policy determined 'the growth of potential output through its influence on the supply side of the economy'.

This new approach to the assignment problem became orthodox in many countries in the 1980s, but Germany got there 20 years earlier than Britain. As in Germany, Keynesian economics had no significant influence in Japan and relatively little in France. It was in the English-speaking countries – Britain, the United States, Australia and New Zealand – and in Italy where virtually all academic economists take their higher degrees in English-speaking universities, and Sweden where English superseded the German in which Wicksell published after 1918, that the Keynesian approach to economic policy had most influence. These have all, in some cases painfully, had to adopt the very different policy framework which Giersch and Helmstädter describe. In his article in this volume, Budd documents the collapse in Britain of the Keynesian paradigm as a foundation for macroeconomic policy.

But there are questions which need to be answered before it can be finally assumed that developments in the world economy in the 1960s and the 1970s have decisively shown that the Keynesian approach to macroeconomic policy no longer has anything practical to contribute.

In particular, its remarkable success in the 1950s needs to be explained. Budd says rightly that Friedman's presidential address, 'The role of monetary policy' (Friedman, 1968) can reasonably be described as 'the most important contribution to the employment debate in the post war period' (see p. 128).

Friedman has provided the basis for the new paradigm that succeeded the Keynesian one. Its explanation of the collapse of naive Keynesian policy into inflation followed by stagflation as countries sought to maintain unemployment below the 'natural' or microeconomic Walrasian equilibrium rate has appeared highly plausible. But there are two questions about this new post-Keynesian orthodoxy.

The first is how the Friedman approach would explain the 1950s. In Britain inflation fell continuously from 1951 until 1959, so unemployment presumably exceeded the 'natural' rate in most of the decade. But British unemployment was below 2 per cent and often below 1½ per cent. Is there a convincing microeconomic explanation of why equilibrium unemployment was so incredibly low in the 1950s? We know all about the failures of naive Keynesianism in the 1960s and the 1970s which led to its abandonment, but its extraordinary success in the 1950s remains to be explained in the language of the new Friedman and post-Friedman paradigm. I shall attempt an explanation in the concluding section of this chapter.

The second question about the apparent success of the Friedman paradigm is how this explains the involuntary unemployment of the 1930s which provided the opening for Keynes and Keynesianism. Was there involuntary unemployment then in the sense that there were workers who would take work if it became available at the current wage, even if prices rose a little? All commentators agree that such unemployment evidently existed. Translating into Friedman's language, the Walrasian equilibrium at which unemployment would have been at its 'natural rate' in the 1930s will have been far lower than actual unemployment. But how many years would it have taken market forces to get within sight of the natural rate? If the Walrasian equilibrium was intolerably distant, was there not a case for an active policy approach subsequently labelled 'Keynesian' which would seek to get close to the natural rate more rapidly than market forces. Ricardo would have said no. Friedman would say no. Malthus would have said yes, as did Keynes and those who supported him.

THE CIVIL SERVANTS AND THE ECONOMISTS

Civil servants are central to the development of actual employment policy in Chapters 3, 4 and 5. Is that surprising? Civil servants advise ministers who are and always have been extremely concerned by the economic condition of those they govern. It is therefore the responsibility of the Civil Service to be utterly aware of all *practical* means by which the social welfare of populations can be advanced, and discontents ameliorated. Employment and the consequent opportunity to obtain income by working for it is universally recognized as one of the most important elements in social welfare. Ministers of all parties wish to reduce unemployment because this will raise the welfare of the families they represent, be electorally advantageous and reduce social unrest. The civil servants who advise ministers will need to be fully aware of the costs of alternative means to reduce unemployment because higher taxation or higher interest rates will have social opportunity costs, so they will actually present ministers with a balance sheet.

They are not less qualified to do this than the academic economics profession. They are not even necessarily less qualified in academic economics. In the periods about which Harris (Chapter 3) and Peden (Chapter 4) write, many professors and lecturers in economics came into the subject without degrees in economics. Appointment to economics posts with degrees in history, classics and mathematics was common in the late-19th and early-20th centuries, when, as Peden's Chapter 4 makes very clear, there was at least an examination paper in economics for entrants to the administrative grade of the Civil Service for which some candidates prepared. Two examples of the most distinguished British academic economists who began their university careers in the 1920s are John Hicks and Roy Harrod. Hicks took a politics, philosophy and economics degree in Balliol College, Oxford in 1925, and he has written that 'My tutor in economics was a military historian, who had no interest in the subject and failed to awaken any in me. I turned to economics after I had taken my degree, through a fortunate contact I had with Graham Wallas, and through him with LSE' (Hicks, 1977, p. 134). Harrod was elected to a permanent Oxford teaching post in economics in 1923 without having taken an economics examination of any kind. He took First Class Honours degrees in classical literature, ancient history and philosophy (Greats) and after that in modern history (Harrod, 1951, p. 317). Harrod's technical qualifications as an economist on his first appointment were weaker than those of the senior civil servants of the 1920s and the 1930s whose qualifications Peden outlines. After that the economic knowledge of Harrod, Hicks and the civil servants grew as their careers developed.

In the course of their careers, many academic economists acquire ability and experience in what Sir Michael Postan has described as the special strength of our subject, the ability to draw far-reaching conclusions from a narrow range of fact. Some of the greatest economic theorists have relied on what Nicholas Kaldor has described as 'stylised facts', broad historical generalizations about data. An illustration is his statement in the Cambridge Political Economy Club that, in the previous two centuries in Britain, money wages had never fallen, or in print that the capital output ratio, the rate of profit and the share of profits had all been constant in Britain and the United States for a century (Kaldor, 1957 [1960], p. 260). The ability to take stylized facts far can produce a new economic paradigm when the existing one contradicts elementary data.

The Civil Service will be especially careful that nothing it advises a minister to say contradicts facts of any kind. Thus a minister who wished to repeat Kaldor's remark about the downward stickiness of money wages would be reminded that they fell 30 per cent between 1921 and 1923.

For an academic economist it is generally acceptable to repeat statistics derived by others with a proper acknowledgement of their responsibility for what is cited. For a minister to get it wrong because someone on whose evidence he or she has relied has erred is not acceptable. The statistics civil servants prepare for ministers are therefore far more cautiously presented and derived than those which some of the greatest economists deploy. Most members of the academic economics profession derive, prepare and present data with care, objectivity and the sophisticated expertise of modern econometrics, but this has not always been the case with the greatest and most original economic theorists.

Ministers have a particular obligation to implement policies which work. Since financial markets influence the outcome of policies, it is scarcely surprising that the Treasury of the 1920s and the 1930s took a great deal of advice from the City of London and the Bank of England. In contrast, Keynes could ignore the influence of financial markets when it suited him. The theory of the determination of the rate of interest which is a central element in the *General Theory* took no account of the influence of international interest rates on the interest rate in London because the book describes a closed economy. In 1936, Joan Robinson wished to include a chapter on the relationship between British and foreign interest rates in her *Essays in the Theory of Employment* (Robinson, 1937). She sent Keynes the proofs of the chapter and he responded:

> I beg you not to publish ... You do not seem to realize that if you are right the whole theory of liquidity preference has to be thrown overboard. The rate of interest on English money no longer depends on the quantity of English money and the liquidity preference of the holders of it. (Keynes, 1973, vol. 14, p. 146)

Joan Robinson complied and told Keynes four days later, 'I finally decided to cut all the controversial matter out of my exchange essay' (Ibid., p. 147). This illustrates how the greatest academic economists can suppress the influence of international markets from their theories and sometimes also those published by others. For chancellors, international markets are all too liable to prove 'judge and jury' of the effectiveness of their policies. Hence Peden's account of the way in which the Treasury took advice from the City and the Bank of England which even overrode that of Hawtrey, its sole academic economist, shows that the Civil Service was doing precisely the job it was appointed to do, to give effective advice to the chancellor, which would not wrong-foot him or the economy.

The advice of civil servants which has to take everything of significance into account might often appear untidy and unappealing if it was presented to academic journal editors, but ministers would be ill-advised if they based their decisions on elegantly presented articles which omitted some of the most significant practical considerations.

This suggests that the particular contribution of economists is to create new and more penetrating analytical frameworks for the examination of practical issues when significant changes in the underlying foundations of thought are required. They will also be aware of important new work in the universities, and convey this in a comprehensible and operational form to those who give the advice on which decisions are based. But they do not have skills and insights into what policy should be which exceed those of civil servants who opened their careers with similar academic qualifications and have followed these with 20 to 30 years of practical experience.

It is therefore in no way surprising that in the period Harris describes, civil servants made stronger contributions to the reduction of unemployment than academic economists. The same underlying framework of analysis was common to both, and civil servants were closer to the details of practical policy. In the period on which Peden focuses, the framework of analysis which guided the Treasury had become inappropriate so there was a genuine task for academic economists, but the new theory with which Keynes filled this gap rested on assumptions which were so limiting that it is not clear that better policies would have resulted in the 1930s if the influence of Keynesian economists had been as powerful as it subsequently became.

After 1945, as Budd explains, it was agreed that the size and influence of the economic section of the Treasury should be greatly extended. In 1939 there was just one civil servant employed specifically as an economist, Hawtrey in the Treasury. In 1995 the government economic service employs more than 500 economists but their separation from the mainstream administrative Civil Service is gradually diminishing. Members of the economic service can be considered for the most senior administrative posts in all government departments and several have become deputy secretaries with opportunities for further promotion. All administrative civil servants attend several intense economics courses during their careers and this is bringing Britain closer to the French system where all senior civil servants have some economics, and where there are no specialist economists who never administer. In addition, Britain like Germany now has its 'wise men' (six instead of the German three) and a panel of academic economists advises regularly on the Treasury model which guides macroeconomic policy decisions.

There is therefore a growing recognition of what is evident from the chapters in this book, that it is desirable that civil servants should be fully aware of relevant academic work which needs to be tempered with a detailed grasp of actual empirical influences.

So far as the explanation and reduction of unemployment is concerned, further work is now needed from those whose principal contribution is theoretical because few will be content with a state of affairs where the equilibrium rate of unemployment is as high as two million. At the same time, the mainstream Civil Service will have most expertise on detailed labour market policies to reduce the apparent Walrasian equilibrium rate of unemployment of 8 per cent. The final section of this chapter will be concerned with the ways forward, where Budd indicates that much remains to be done.

UNEMPLOYMENT: A WAY FORWARD

The real puzzle is why unemployment of around 2 per cent was able to produce falling inflation in the 1950s when it has taken unemployment of at least 8 and sometimes 10 per cent to produce this result in the 1980s and the 1990s. Those satisfied with Friedman's framework must respond that for microeconomic reasons, the Walrasian natural rate was less than 2 per cent in the 1950s and more than 8 per cent in the 1980s.

The most direct resolution of that paradox is the hysteresis literature which indicates that there are significant considerations in an economy which cause the natural rate of unemployment to track the actual rate. As David Worswick has commented, 'as unemployment has risen from 2 to 3 to 5 to 7 per cent, with inflation sometimes accelerating and sometimes slowing down, the "natural rate" has been puffing and panting trying to keep up' (1981, p. 14). Worswick's comment can be placed alongside OECD estimates of the British natural rate of unemployment.[3] In 1971 actual unemployment was 3.4 per cent and the OECD estimate of the natural rate was 2.6 per cent; in 1975 actual unemployment was 4.1 per cent and the natural rate 4.0 per cent; in 1980 actual unemployment was 7.2 per cent and the natural rate 7.4 per cent; in 1985 actual unemployment was 11.2 per cent and the natural rate 10.2 per cent; in 1990 the actual rate of unemployment was 8.8 per cent and the natural rate 8.4 per cent; and in 1995 the actual rate is 8.7 per cent and the natural rate 7.7 per cent. In 1979 when Mrs Thatcher became prime minister the OECD estimate of the natural rate was 6.6 per cent and it apparently rose to 7.7 per cent in the following 16 years of Conservative government despite the vast range of microeconomic policies to make the labour market more competitive including substantial reductions in unemployment benefits relative to earnings and a variety of policy changes to reduce union power. There are evidently powerful forces which cause the Walrasian equilibrium rate of unemployment to track actual unemployment upwards and downwards. But if the natural rate of unemployment moves with the actual rate, there is a clear underlying potential for Keynesian employment policies, because if these succeed in bringing actual unemployment down, they should also exert downward influence on the Walrasian equilibrium rate.

That downward pressure will be extremely gradual. The most plausible social and economic explanation of an adjustment of the equilibrium unemployment rate to the actual rate is that some of the elements which combine to produce the Walrasian equilibrium rate have a social content.

In the 1950s there had been virtually 100 per cent employment for more than a decade. Social attitudes adjusted to the knowledge that everyone had a job. Living off social benefits which few found necessary could therefore be regarded as aberrant social behaviour which few were tempted to embark on. Because jobs were universally available with more vacancies than unemployed in 1950, 1951, 1954, 1955 and 1956, those who administered the benefit system felt able to apply it rigorously.

In the 1980s, in contrast, as the population became accustomed to 10 per cent unemployment with far higher rates in depressed regions, it was widely accepted that, as in the 1920s and the 1930s, many with the strongest personal desire to work would actually be unemployed for long periods. Living off benefits therefore became inescapable for many families, and those who administered the system became fully aware of this.

An economy can settle at very different unemployment rates and behave as if these are long-term equilibria, when they are merely temporary equilibria which can be transformed by changes in attitudes and behaviour.

But the transitory equilibria can only be modified slowly and gradually. If two million families have become accustomed to living off benefits, and economic conditions change so that a quarter of a million can move into remunerative employment, some will only leave the benefits system to which they have adjusted their lives if the financial rewards are very considerable. As more jobs become available, many who are unemployed will eagerly take newly available jobs and the attitudes of those who make no effort to find employment will slowly appear less acceptable to those who administer social welfare and within the various social milieu to which the unemployed belong. Changes in attitude are achievable, and unemployment will become less acceptable the less of it there is.

This indicates that observed natural rates of unemployment will be lower in societies which manage to bring their actual rates of unemployment down in a manner which does not produce an acceleration of inflation which forces the rapid reversal of reflationary policies.

The policy approach which will then be required to achieve a long-term reduction in the natural and actual rates of unemployment will need detailed work of four kinds, some of which are outlined by Budd:

1. A greater understanding of the behaviour of insiders/outsiders in the labour market.
2. Policies to churn unemployment.
3. A flexible administration of social welfare/benefit systems.
4. Demand must grow gradually enough to allow social attitudes to change.

A Greater Understanding of the Behaviour of Insiders/Outsiders in the Labour Market

The academic work on the market behaviour of 'insiders', those who are continually in work, and 'outsiders', those in danger of being in nearly-continual unemployment, who may go on to become accustomed to a way of life in which work is of peripheral importance, needs to be more thoroughly understood in the academic literature. Corry and Budd refer to several academic economists who are doing important work in this highly fashionable area.

Policies to Churn Unemployment

Those concerned with government labour market policies will need to continue to develop policies which produce a churning of unemployment to prevent the individual unemployed from settling into perpetual unemployment.[4] Many of the detailed policies which Budd describes have this characteristic and they are constantly being developed. This work by civil servants is of the detailed kind that the 19th-century civil servants whom Harris describes performed, and civil servants will inevitably be those who do it. It will be surprising if academic articles concerning the churning of unemployment are seriously considered by journal editors, but this is an essential element in a strategy to change social behaviour so as to bring the natural rate of unemployment back towards the levels of the 1950s.

A Flexible Administration of Social Welfare/Benefit Systems

Those who administer social welfare will need to tighten the various rules and conditions on which payments are available when, as in the 1950s, work is easily found. Conversely, they will need to relax the rigours of enforcement in periods where there are many who cannot possibly find work at socially acceptable rates of pay. That again is essentially a task for the civil service. The dichotomy Harris describes of the 1860s between a 'delinquent underclass of "professional" unemployed who made a living from begging and exploitation of charity, and a class of "virtuous" unemployed who were the victims of unpredictable industrial misfortune' (p. 62) has always been present in the official mind, but the two classes have not been administratively distinguishable. They are never likely to be, but much can be done if the strategic intention is to administer benefit systems in a manner which reflects the availability of work.

Demand Must Grow Gradually Enough to Allow Social Attitudes to Change

The pressure of demand on resources can be raised but only at the slow rate at which social attitudes change. British demand-expansion used to take the form of rapid simultaneous increases in private and public consumption (as taxes were reduced and public expenditure increased), in exports (as low interest rates to encourage expansion produced weaknesses in sterling) and in investment as higher consumption and exports created shortages of physical capital. With consumption, investment and exports all expanding rapidly at the same time, short-term growth rose to unsustainable rates of 6 to 8 per cent, imports and inflation soared and expansion had to be sharply halted within less than two years. Such brief and unsustainable bursts of demand expansion discredited naive Keynesianism in the 1960s and the 1970s, and it offered too little scope to produce the changes in social attitudes to unemployment which might have brought the natural rate down. What is needed is sustained expansion at a rate slightly faster than the one which most regard as the underlying rate of growth of the economy. How to achieve this is continually discussed in the academic literature and by city economists.

A combination of a deeper academic understanding of hysteresis, a churning of unemployment to prevent it from sticking, a flexible administration of social welfare, and demand-management which is expansionist but only slightly so are all directions in which policy to return unemployment to the levels of the 1950s could develop.

NOTES

1. The questions discussed in the Policy Economy Club from its foundation until 1921, its membership, and a few memoirs of its meetings are set out in Political Economy Club (1921).
2. I published a similar description of Kahn's multiplier in Eltis (1979, p. 126), 'the concept which taught two generations of English speaking economists that you can expand your cake and eat it faster at the same time'.
3. These are estimates of the non accelerating wage rate of unemployment or NAWRU.
4. The unemployed may be dividable into U_a, the effectively employable, and U_b, those who have been unemployed for so long that employers regard them as no longer employable. Many of the U_b employees will have actively ceased to seek work. If equilibrium in the labour market requires the potential availability of U_n unemployed workers for work, U_n will equal U_a when unemployment is at the natural rate, and the total level of unemployment when the labour market is in equilibrium will be $(U_n + U_b)$. If U_b can be reduced by churning, for instance by offering training or temporary work to those who despair of re-employment, they will become re-employable for a time, even if their temporary work

ceases, and therefore switch from the U_b to the U_a pool of unemployment. This will reduce $(U_n + U_b)$ overall unemployment when the labour market is in equilibrium.

REFERENCES

Cannan, E. (1894), 'Employment', in R.H. Inglis Palgrave (ed.), *Dictionary of Political Economy*, vol. 1, London: Macmillan.

Casson, M. (1983), *The Economics of Unemployment: An Historical Perspective*, Oxford: Martin Robertson.

Eatwell, J., Milgate, M. and Newman, P. (eds) (1987), *The New Palgrave Dictionary of Economics*, 4 vols, London: Macmillan.

Eltis, W. (1979), 'How Rapid Public Sector Growth can Undermine the Growth of the National Product', in W. Beckerman (ed.), *Slow Growth in Britain: Causes and Consequences*, Oxford: Oxford University Press.

Friedman, M. (1968), 'The Role of Monetary Policy', *American Economic Review*, **58**, March.

Giersch, H. (1986), 'Economics as a Public Good', *Banca Nationale Del Lavoro Quarterly Review*, **158**, September.

Harris, J. (1972), *Unemployment and Politics: A Study in British Social Policy*, Oxford: Clarendon Press.

Harris, J. (1977), *William Beveridge: A Biography*, Oxford: Oxford University Press.

Harrod, R.F. (1951), *The Life of John Maynard Keynes*, London: Macmillan.

Helmstädter, E. (1988), 'The Irrelevance of Keynes to German Economic Policy', in W. Eltis and P. Sinclair (eds), *Keynes and Economic Policy: The Relevance of the General Theory after Fifty Years*, Basingstoke: Macmillan.

Hicks, J. (1977), 'Recollections and Documents', in *Economic Perspectives: Further Essays on Money and Growth*, Oxford: University Press.

Hutchison, T. (1988), *Before Adam Smith: The Emergence of Political Economy 1662–1776*, Oxford: Basil Blackwell.

Kahn, R. (1931), 'The Relation of Home Investment to Unemployment', *Economic Journal*, **41**, June.

Kaldor, N. (1957), 'A Model of Economic Growth', *Economic Journal*, **67**, December. Reprinted in 1960 in *Essays in Economic Stability and Growth*, London: Duckworth, 259–300.

Keynes, J.M. (1936, 1973), *The General Theory of Employment, Interest and Money*, London: Macmillan. Reprinted as vol. 7 of *The Collected Writings of John Maynard Keynes*, London: Macmillan.

Keynes, J.M. (1973), *The General Theory and After*, vols 13–14 of *The Collected Writings of John Maynard Keynes*, London: Macmillan.

Malthus, T.R. (1820), *Principles of Political Economy*, London: John Murray.

Palgrave, R.J.I. (ed) (1894–1900), *Dictionary of Political Economy*, 3 vols, London: Macmillan.

Political Economy Club (1921), *Centenary Volume*, London: Macmillan.

Ricardo, D. (1951), *Notes on Malthus's Principles of Political Economy*, vol. II of *The Works and Correspondence of David Ricardo*, Cambridge: Cambridge University Press.

Ricardo, D. (1952a), *Speeches and Evidence*, vol. V of *The Works and Correspondence of David Ricardo*, Cambridge: Cambridge University Press.

Ricardo, D. (1952b), *Letters 1816–1818*, vol. VII of *The Works and Correspondence of David Ricardo*, Cambridge: Cambridge University Press.

Robinson, J. (1937), *Essays in the Theory of Employment*, London: Macmillan.

Worswick, D. (1981), 'The Money Supply and the Exchange Rate', in W.A. Eltis and P.J.N. Sinclair (eds), *The Money Supply and the Exchange Rate*, Oxford: Clarendon Press.

Index